EDEXCEL HISTORY

T0326143

GCSE 9-1

Superpower Relations and the Cold War, 1941–91

by Simon Taylor

SCHOLASTIC

Author Simon Taylor

Series Editor Paul Martin

Reviewer Rosemary Rees

Editorial team Aidan Gill, Turnstone Solutions Limited, Rachel Morgan, Audrey Stokes, Kirsty Taylor, Caroline Low

Typesetting Daniel Prescott, Couper Street Type Co

Cover design Dipa Mistry

App development Hannah Barnett, Phil Crothers and RAIOSOFT International Pvt Ltd

Photographs cover and title page: two butterflies with flags on wings as symbol of relations USA and Soviet Union sunshinesmile/123RF; pages 10 and 11: flags: USSR, Mikhail Mishchenko/Shutterstock; UK, Sunflowerr/Shutterstock; USA, Sunflowerr/Shutterstock Hungary, Magcom/Shutterstock; Cuba, Sunflowerr/Shutterstock; Czech Republic, Sunflowerr/Shutterstock; pages 10 and 16: Joseph Stalin, US Army Signal Corps/Wikimedia Commons; pages 10 and 16: Winston Churchill, BiblioArchives Library Archives/Wikimedia Commons; pages 10, 16 and 19: Harry Truman, National Archives and Records Administration, Office of Presidential Libraries, Harry S. Truman Library/Wikimedia Commons; page 10: Nikita S. Khrushchev, Bundesarchiv Bild/Wikimedia Commons; Imry Nagy, FOTOFORTEPAN Jánosi Katalin adományozó/Wikimedia Commons; John F. Kennedy, National Archives and Records Administration/Wikimedia Commons; pages 11 and 33: Fidel Castro, emkaplin/Shutterstock; pages 11 and 39: Leonid Brezhnev, Commons Bundesarchiv/Wikimedia Commons; page 11: Alexander Dubcek, National Archives (archive.org)/Wikimedia Commons; Jimmy Carter, White House/Wikimedia Commons; pages 11 and 49: Ronald Reagan, Wikimedia Commons; pages 11 and 45: Mikhail Gorbachev, RIA Novosti archive, Vladimir Vyatkin/Wikimedia Commons; pages 14 and 70: Yalta summit, photograph from the Army Signal Corps Collection in the U.S. National Archives/Wikimedia Commons; page 15: Potsdam conference, U.S. Government/Wikimedia Commons; page 30: Berlin Wall, Keystone Press/Alamy Stock Photo; page 32: JFK speech Ich bin ein Berliner, Robert Knudsen, White House/Wikimedia Commons; page 36: Khrushchev and Kennedy shaking hands, National Archives and Records Administration/Wikimedia Commons; page 40: Soviet tanks in Prague, CTK/Alamy Stock Photo; page 43: Nuclear missile silo, Steve Jurvetson from Menlo Park, USA, CC BY 2.0 (httpscreativecommons.orglicensesby2.0)/Wikimedia Commons; page 44: Delta-II class nuclear-powered ballistic missile submarine 2, Wikimedia Commons; page 52: Berlin Wall-Brandenburg Gate, Sue Ream, CC BY 3.0 (httpscreativecommons.orglicensesby3.0)/Wikimedia Commons; page 77: girl sitting exam, Monkey Business Images/Shutterstock

Illustration QBS Learning

Designed using Adobe InDesign

Published in the UK by Scholastic Education, 2020
Book End, Range Road, Witney, Oxfordshire, OX29 0YD
A division of Scholastic Limited
London – New York – Toronto – Sydney – Auckland
Mexico City – New Delhi – Hong Kong
SCHOLASTIC and associated logos are trademarks and/or registered trademarks of Scholastic Inc.
www.scholastic.co.uk

© 2020 Scholastic Limited
1 2 3 4 5 6 7 8 9   0 1 2 3 4 5 6 7 8 9

British Library Cataloguing-in-Publication Data
A catalogue record for this book is available from the British Library.

ISBN 978-1407-18340-4

Printed and bound by Bell and Bain Ltd, Glasgow
Papers used by Scholastic Limited are made from wood grown in sustainable forests.

All rights reserved. This book is sold subject to the condition that it shall not, by way of trade or otherwise, be lent, hired out or otherwise circulated without the publisher's prior consent in any form of binding or cover other than that in which it is published and without a similar condition, including this condition, being imposed upon the subsequent purchaser.

No part of this publication may be reproduced, stored in a retrieval system, or transmitted, in any form or by any means, electronic, mechanical, photocopying, recording or otherwise, other than for the purposes described in the content of this product, without the prior permission of the publisher. This product remains in copyright.

Due to the nature of the web, we cannot guarantee the content or links of any site mentioned.

Every effort has been made to trace copyright holders for the works reproduced in this book, and the publishers apologise for any inadvertent omissions.

Note from the publisher:
Please use this product in conjunction with the official specification and sample assessment materials. Ask your teacher if you are unsure where to find them.

Contents

Check your answers on the free revision app or at www.scholastic.co.uk/gcse

Features of this guide

The best way to retain information is to take an active approach to revision.

Throughout this book, you will find lots of features that will make your revision an active, successful process.

SNAPIT!

Use the Snap it! feature in the revision app to take pictures of key concepts and information. Great for revision on the go!

Regular exercise helps stimulate the brain and will help you relax.

DOIT!
Activities to embed your knowledge and understanding and prepare you for the exams.

Find methods of relaxation that work for you throughout the revision period.

Words shown in **purple bold** can be found in the glossary on page 79.

NAILIT!

Succinct and vital tips on how to do well in your exam.

STRETCHIT!
Provides content that stretches you further.

CHECKIT!
Check your knowledge at the end of a subtopic.

Revise in pairs or small groups and deliver presentations on topics to each other.

PRACTICE PAPERS
Full mock-exam papers to practise before you sit the real thing!

FOR HIGH-MARK QUESTIONS, SPEND TIME **PLANNING** YOUR ANSWER!

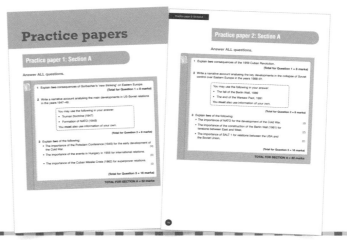

FREE REVISION APP

- The **free revision app** can be downloaded to your mobile phone (iOS and Android), making **on the go revision** easy.

- Use the revision calendar to help map out your revision in the lead-up to the exam.

- Complete multiple-choice questions and create your own SNAP**IT!** revision cards.

www.scholastic.co.uk/gcse

Online answers and additional resources
All of the tasks in this book are designed to get you thinking and to consolidate your understanding through thought and application. Therefore, it is important to write your own answers before checking. Some questions include answer lines where you need to fill in your answer in the book. Other questions require you to use a separate piece of paper so that you can draft your response and work out the best way of answering.

Get plenty of sleep, especially the night before an exam.

LOOK AFTER YOURSELF

Help your brain by looking after your whole body!

Once you have worked through a section, you can check your answers to Do it!, Stretch it!, Check it! and the exam practice papers on the app or at **www.scholastic.co.uk/gcse**.

Topic focus:
Period study

For almost fifty years the USA and the Soviet Union were locked in an epic struggle called the Cold War.

Key topic 1: The origins of the Cold War, 1941–58

The story begins in 1941 when Britain, the USA and the Soviet Union formed a Grand Alliance to defeat Nazi Germany. Key Topic 1 examines how this 'marriage of convenience' steadily unravelled across the Tehran (1943), Yalta (1945) and Potsdam (1945) conferences. As the Second World War ended, therefore, a new Cold War began to emerge between the USA and the Soviet Union. This was partly due to ideological differences and the hostile attitudes of Stalin, Truman and Churchill. The level of mistrust was deepened by the USA's development of the atomic bomb (1945), the creation of Soviet satellite states in Europe (1945–48) and stark diplomatic warnings in the form of the Long and Novikov telegrams (1946).

In 1947 the USA put forward the Truman Doctrine (1947) and the Marshall Plan (1947) to contain further communist expansion. The Soviet Union replied with Cominform (1947) and Comecon (1949). War came close when Stalin tried to blockade Berlin in 1948. The military alliance of NATO (1949) and later the Warsaw Pact (1955) grew out of this crisis. It also gave new impetus to the arms race, which had the potential to destroy humanity. In 1956 a new Soviet leader, Khrushchev, once again flexed Soviet muscle by invading Hungary and crushing its people's hopes of winning freedom from hard line communism.

Key topic 2: Cold War crises, 1958–70

This key topic focuses on three Cold War crises. The first centres on Berlin, a city surrounded by communist East Germany and itself split between East and West. The period 1958–61 witnessed growing superpower tensions, mainly caused by the refugee problem and Khrushchev's Berlin Ultimatum (1958). With the summit meetings of 1959–61 all ending in failure, the communist authorities resorted to building a wall around West Berlin. In so doing, they created one of the Cold War's most powerful symbols.

The next crisis focuses on Cuba, under the leadership of Fidel Castro since the 1959 revolution. His growing friendship with the Soviet Union led to the disastrous US-backed Bay of Pigs incident (1961) followed by the Cuban Missile Crisis (1962), when nuclear war seemed a real possibility. This had the result of scaring the two superpowers into creating a 'hotline' and agreeing treaties such as the Limited Test Ban Treaty (1963) to make the world a safer place.

The final Cold War crisis examines Czechoslovakia's doomed attempt to break free from rigid communist control in 1968. The hope of creating 'socialism with a human face' was met by a Warsaw Pact invasion, the repressive Brezhnev Doctrine and a lacklustre response from the West.

Key topic 3: The end of the Cold War, 1970–91

The final key topic begins with efforts in the 1970s to reduce tensions between the superpowers. This process of détente led to SALT 1 (1972), the Helsinki Agreement (1975) and SALT 2 (1979). However the Soviet invasion of Afghanistan (1979) triggered the 'Second Cold War'. President Carter issued the Carter Doctrine and boycotted the Moscow Olympics (1980). The next president, Reagan, went further by turning science fiction into reality with the Strategic Defence Initiative (SDI).

From 1985, Cold War politics was transformed by the arrival of Mikhail Gorbachev, a new style Soviet leader. He worked with Reagan to agree the Intermediate-Range Nuclear Force (INF) Treaty (1987), ending the arms race. Gorbachev's 'new thinking' saw the Berlin Wall fall in 1989 and communism removed from Eastern Europe. In 1991 another symbol of the Cold War, the Warsaw Pact, dissolved. The final act was the break up of the Soviet Union itself in 1991. This brought a formal end to the Cold War.

Timeline

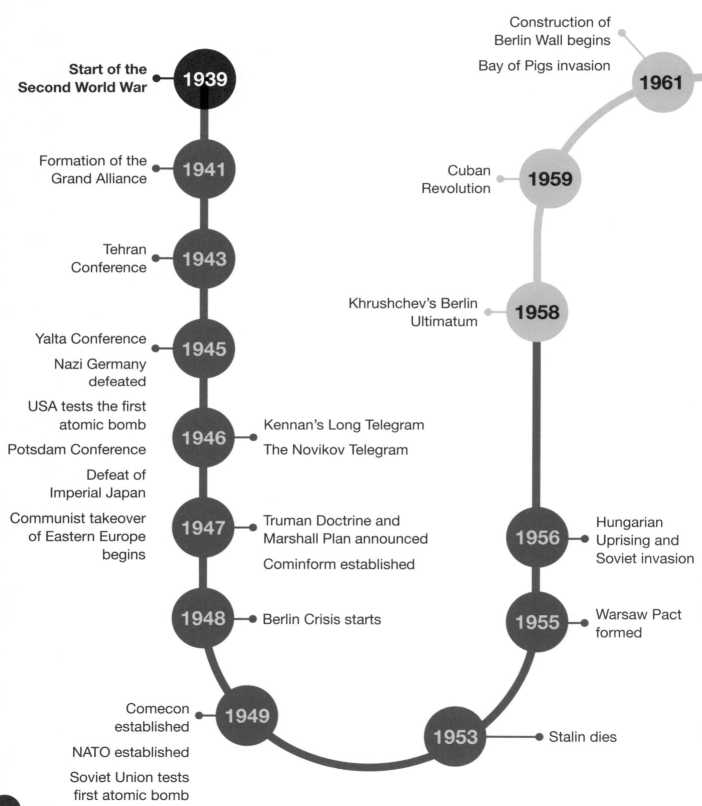

Start of the Second World War — **1939**

Formation of the Grand Alliance — 1941

Tehran Conference — 1943

Yalta Conference

Nazi Germany defeated — 1945

USA tests the first atomic bomb

Potsdam Conference — 1946 — Kennan's Long Telegram

The Novikov Telegram

Defeat of Imperial Japan

Communist takeover of Eastern Europe begins — 1947 — Truman Doctrine and Marshall Plan announced

Cominform established

1948 — Berlin Crisis starts

Comecon established

NATO established — 1949

Soviet Union tests first atomic bomb

1953 — Stalin dies

Warsaw Pact formed — 1955

Hungarian Uprising and Soviet invasion — 1956

Khrushchev's Berlin Ultimatum — 1958

Cuban Revolution — 1959

Construction of Berlin Wall begins

Bay of Pigs invasion — 1961

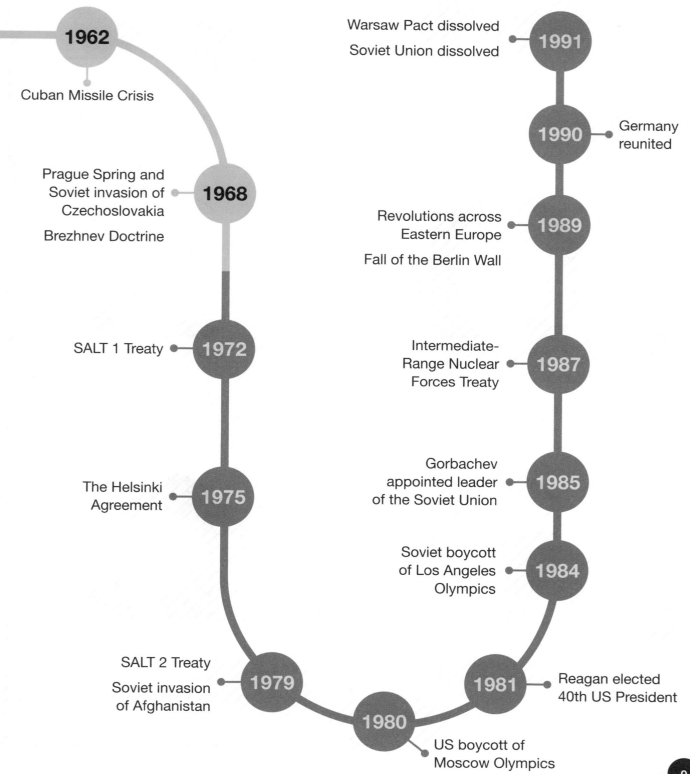

Alliance, expansion and containment. Military alliance in Second World War, followed by Soviet Union trying to expand communist ideology; USA trying to contain the spread of communism

Escalation – rise in tension between the Soviet Union and USA

Détente, flash points and collapse – a mixed time in the Cold War, with periods of high tension and improved relations

1962
Cuban Missile Crisis

Prague Spring and Soviet invasion of Czechoslovakia

Brezhnev Doctrine

1968

SALT 1 Treaty — **1972**

The Helsinki Agreement — **1975**

SALT 2 Treaty

Soviet invasion of Afghanistan — **1979**

1980

US boycott of Moscow Olympics

1981 — Reagan elected 40th US President

Warsaw Pact dissolved

Soviet Union dissolved — **1991**

1990 — Germany reunited

Revolutions across Eastern Europe

Fall of the Berlin Wall — **1989**

Intermediate-Range Nuclear Forces Treaty — **1987**

Gorbachev appointed leader of the Soviet Union — **1985**

Soviet boycott of Los Angeles Olympics — **1984**

Key figures

Joseph Stalin

The Soviet Union's brutal communist leader from the late 1920s until 1953. His fear and hatred of the West was a key reason for the early Cold War.

Winston Churchill

Britain's wartime prime minister from 1940–45. Deeply traditional, he supported the British Empire, hated communism and distrusted Stalin.

Harry Truman

A fierce anti-communist and US President from 1945–53. He played a key role in starting the Cold War, famously saying 'I'm tired of babying the Soviets'.

Nikita Khrushchev

Leader of the Soviet Union from 1955–64. His Cold War credentials include crushing the Hungarian Uprising, building the Berlin Wall and provoking the Cuban Missile Crisis.

Imry Nagy

A popular, reform-minded communist who led Hungary's doomed attempt to break free from Soviet domination. As punishment, Nagy was executed by the Soviets, his body dumped in an unmarked grave.

John F. Kennedy

The young, charismatic US president, assassinated in 1963. Although relatively inexperienced in foreign affairs, Kennedy was keen to prove his Cold War metal by standing up to the Soviets in the Cuban Missile Crisis.

Fidel Castro

The khaki-wearing, cigar-loving communist revolutionary who led Cuba from 1959–2008. His decision to allow Soviet nuclear missiles on Cuba almost started a third World War.

Leonid Brezhnev

Highly decorated Soviet leader from 1964–82, he had 100 medals, mostly awarded by himself. Brezhnev invaded Czechoslovakia and Afghanistan, but also supported détente.

Alexander Dubček

The communist leader of Czechoslovakia for a brief period in 1968. A believer in a 'kinder' version of communism, Dubček initiated the Prague Spring, only to see its ideals crushed by Soviet tanks.

Jimmy Carter

A one-time peanut farmer, Carter served as US President from 1977–81. He wanted to improve relations with the Soviet Union, but the Soviet invasion of Afghanistan forced him to 'get tough'.

Ronald Reagan

A former film star, Reagan served as US President from 1981–89. He felt destroying communism was his God-given duty. Despite this, he ended up working closely with the Soviets.

Mikhail Gorbachev

The son of a peasant, he became the last leader of the Soviet Union, in office from 1985–91. He initiated a series of reforms that would help end the Cold War.

Part One:
The origins of the Cold War 1941–58

Early tension between East and West

The ideological differences between the superpowers

In a hot war, countries fight each other directly. However, for almost 50 years the USA and the Soviet Union were locked in a tense standoff known as the Cold War. They competed with each other in almost every area of life. At the heart of this cold conflict were two very different ways of looking at the world:

	Communism (Soviet Union)	Capitalism (USA)
Political parties	Only the Communist Party is allowed.	Numerous political parties compete with each other.
Elections	No democratic elections. Communist rule cannot be changed.	Governments are chosen in regular democratic elections.
Economy	The state directs the running of the economy. All businesses and factories are state-owned.	People can freely set up businesses and make money. The state does not interfere.
Employment	Everybody is provided with a job.	Employment varies depending on economic performance. It is not for the state to provide.
Equality	Everyone is considered equal. Living standards are broadly similar, with no extremes.	Equality of opportunity, not outcome. There are big differences in wealth.
Rights	Obedience to the state is more important than individual rights. Strict controls exist over what people can say or write.	Individual rights such as freedom of speech and the press are protected.

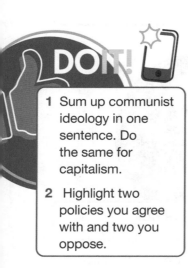

1 Sum up communist ideology in one sentence. Do the same for capitalism.

2 Highlight two policies you agree with and two you oppose.

The Grand Alliance

During the Second World War, Britain, the Soviet Union and the United States worked together as allies to defeat Nazi Germany. The leaders met only three times: at Tehran, Yalta and Potsdam.

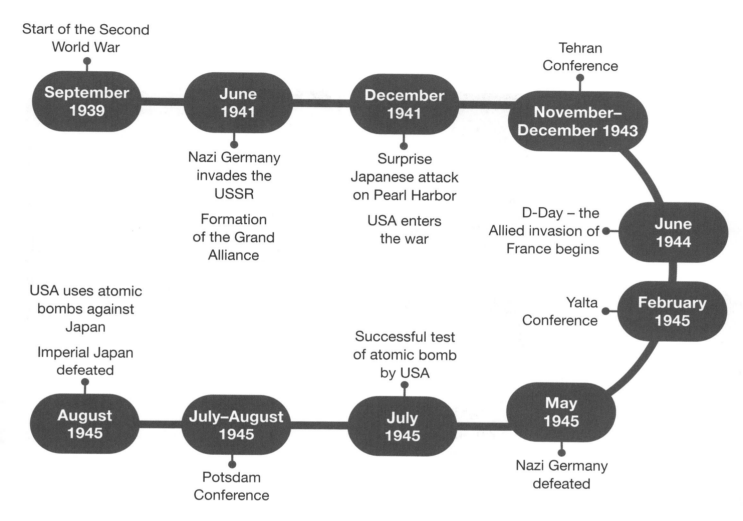

Start of the Second World War

September 1939

June 1941

Nazi Germany invades the USSR

Formation of the Grand Alliance

December 1941

Surprise Japanese attack on Pearl Harbor

USA enters the war

Tehran Conference

November– December 1943

D-Day – the Allied invasion of France begins

June 1944

Yalta Conference

February 1945

USA uses atomic bombs against Japan

Imperial Japan defeated

August 1945

July–August 1945

Potsdam Conference

Successful test of atomic bomb by USA

July 1945

May 1945

Nazi Germany defeated

The Tehran Conference, 1943

The Tehran Conference was the first meeting of the 'Big Three': Stalin, Churchill and Roosevelt. The main aim was to plan the opening of a second front against Germany in Europe. Stalin desperately needed this because his troops were carrying out the majority of the fighting and suffering huge losses.

Tehran agreements

✓ The USA and Britain would invade France by May 1944.

✓ All three countries would keep fighting until Germany surrendered unconditionally. No separate peace deals would be signed.

✓ Once Germany was defeated, the USSR would join the USA and Britain in the war against Japan.

✓ Poland's borders would be moved westwards. It would lose land to the Soviet Union, but gain territory from Germany.

✓ A new international organisation would be set up to promote international peace and cooperation.

NAILIT!

Make sure you know both the main agreements and disagreements at the Tehran, Yalta and Potsdam conferences.

The Yalta Conference, 1945

In February 1945, Churchill, Roosevelt and Stalin met again at Yalta in the Soviet Union. With an Allied victory looking certain, the aim of the conference was to decide on final military strategy and settle the post-war future of Europe. The meeting was reasonably friendly and many agreements were made. However, behind the scenes tension was growing, particularly about **reparations** and Poland. On their return home, Churchill and Roosevelt were criticised for giving away too much to the Soviets.

Agreements (✓) and disagreements (✗) at the Yalta Conference

✓ Germany would be divided into four zones: Soviet, American, British and French.

✓ Like Germany, Berlin would be split into four zones.

✓ Nazi war criminals would be hunted down and put on trial.

✓ Eastern Europe would be in the Soviet Union's 'sphere of influence'.

✓ All countries freed from Nazi control would hold free, democratic elections to choose their new governments.

✓ The Soviet Union would join the war against Japan following Germany's defeat.

✓ A new United Nations organisation would be set up.

✗ Stalin wanted Poland's new provisional government to be mainly loyal communists, known as the 'Lublin Poles'. In contrast, Britain wanted it to contain many Polish leaders who had spent much of the war in Britain, known as the 'London Poles'.

✗ Stalin wanted the Polish/German border to be much further west than either Roosevelt or Churchill.

✗ Stalin wanted Germany to pay huge reparations, but Roosevelt and Churchill worried about the effect of crippling the German economy.

STRETCHIT!

To help understand why Stalin wanted Germany to pay large reparations, carry out further research into the terrible losses suffered by the Soviet Union during the Second World War.

The Potsdam Conference, 1945

The final meeting of the 'Big Three' took place just outside Berlin, at Potsdam. The aim was to finalise the post-war settlement and put into action all of the things agreed at Yalta. Part way through, Churchill was replaced by Clement Attlee as British prime minister, but Attlee made little impact on proceedings. Three factors meant the conference was not successful.

1 A new US President

Roosevelt had died and America's new President, Truman, hated communism. Whereas FDR wanted to cooperate with the Soviet Union, Truman did not see this as important. He took this new 'get tough' stance into the conference, saying 'I'm tired of babying the Soviets'.

2 The atomic bomb

Just before the conference, the USA successfully tested an atomic bomb. Truman personally informed Stalin, who was furious for not being told about its existence earlier (although he actually knew about it from his spies). He now felt threatened by America.

3 Eastern Europe

The British and US governments were angry that Stalin was not allowing free elections in Eastern Europe. They also worried that the huge number of **Red Army** troops in Eastern Europe would become an army of occupation.

DO IT!

1 Write a catchy newspaper headline to sum up the overall result of each of the three wartime conferences.

2 Create a revision poster showing how and why relations between the 'Big Three' changed over the Tehran, Yalta and Potsdam conferences. Be as visual as you can.

✓ Germany and Berlin would be divided into four zones of occupation.

✓ Germany would be de-Nazified: the Nazi Party would be banned, leading Nazis tried for war crimes and democracy re-established.

✓ The United Nations would be set up with the 'Big Three' all playing a full role.

✓ Poland's borders would be moved westwards into Germany, to the rivers Oder and Neisse.

✓ Germany would pay reparations in the form of industrial equipment and materials. Most would go to the Soviet Union.

Agreements (✓) and disagreements (✗) at the Potsdam Conference

✗ Truman opposed the massive reparations bill demanded by Stalin.

✗ Truman wanted free elections to take place in Eastern Europe. Stalin refused to agree.

✗ The West was not happy with the composition of Poland's provisional government, as it was dominated by communists.

The attitudes of Stalin, Truman and Churchill

As Stalin, Truman and Churchill all played a role in developing the Cold War, it is important to understand how they viewed events at the time.

Stalin had little faith in the West. In his view the United States and Britain:

- hated communism
- had deliberately delayed launching the second front in Europe, so Nazi Germany could cause maximum damage in the East
- would invade the Soviet Union at some point in the future.

In addition, the Soviet Union lost 20 million people in the war. Stalin's priority was therefore security. He wanted to gain control over Eastern Europe so it would act as a 'buffer zone' against any future attacks.

Truman disliked Stalin and hated communism. Stalin, he believed, wanted to aggressively spread communism around the world, starting in Eastern Europe.

Truman believed tough talk was the best way to negotiate with Stalin and felt that America's **nuclear monopoly** gave him an advantage. The atomic bombing of Hiroshima and Nagasaki in August 1945 was partly done to demonstrate US military might and to 'scare' Stalin.

Churchill opposed communism and viewed Stalin as a monstrous dictator. He worried about Stalin's plan for Poland. This was because Britain had gone to war on behalf of Polish independence in 1939.

However, by the end of the war, Britain was bankrupt and exhausted. Churchill realised that his ability to influence events in Eastern Europe was limited – what Stalin wanted, he could take.

The creation of Soviet satellite states

In order to create this 'buffer zone' of security, between 1945 and 1948 Stalin took over Eastern Europe, creating **satellite states** under the control of the Soviet Union.

The Communist takeover of a country in Eastern Europe usually began when Communists joined a **coalition government** there. They would take key jobs such as running the police and army, and gradually remove any political opponents. When there were hardly any opponents left, an election would be held – and the Communists would win, setting up a '**people's democracy**'.

The Communist Party took power in Poland and Hungary in 1947, and in Czechoslovakia in 1948.

Poland (1947)

- A coalition government was formed in 1945.
- The Soviet Union used its large military presence to arrest many non-communist leaders, mainly on false charges of collaborating with Germany in the war; 16 politicians were placed on trial in Moscow and imprisoned.
- In 1947 the Communist Party won a majority in rigged elections.

Hungary (1947)

- In the 1945 election the Communist Party, led by Rakosi, gained only 17 per cent of the vote.
- Pressure from the Soviet Union meant that the Communist Party was invited into a coalition government and given key roles, including control of the security police. This gave Rakosi the means to start arresting political opponents.
- The communists won the 1947 election after a campaign of intimidation. All other political parties were then banned.

The impact on US-Soviet relations

In the West, Stalin's actions were greeted with anger and fear. This was conveyed by Winston Churchill in 1946 during a speech at Fulton, Missouri, in the USA where he stated:

- The Soviet Union was a threat to freedom and world peace and was determined to spread communism around the world.

- Eastern Europe was falling under Soviet control, creating an 'Iron Curtain' between the capitalist West and communist East.

- Britain and the USA should form a 'special relationship' to stop further Soviet expansion.

Distrust between the two sides was growing. Stalin saw the speech as provocative, calling it a 'declaration of war' and accusing Churchill of 'warmongering'.

	Territory gained by USSR in 1945
	Countries under communist control
	Yugoslavia: communist but independent
	Iron curtain

The division of Eastern and Western Europe by 1949

Czechoslovakia (1948)

- The Communist Party had genuine support, winning 38 per cent of the vote in the 1946 election. Lacking a majority, they entered into a coalition government.
- In 1948, in a move approved by Stalin, the communists seized total power. Opposition politicians were arrested or murdered. Foreign minister Jan Masaryk, for example, was thrown from his office window.

DOIT!

Compile a factsheet about Hungary and Czechoslovakia in the Cold War as you work through this revision guide. Include sections on
1) how the communists gained power,
2) attempted uprisings, 3) independence.

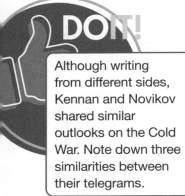

DO IT!

Although writing from different sides, Kennan and Novikov shared similar outlooks on the Cold War. Note down three similarities between their telegrams.

The Long and Novikov telegrams

As international tensions started to rise following the end of the war, the USA and Soviet Union both wanted to know what the other was up to. Senior **diplomats** were asked to provide insights.

In 1946 George Kennan was a senior official in the US **Embassy** in Moscow. His 8000 word 'Long Telegram' had a major impact on US-Soviet relations because it was a key influence in developing President Truman's policy of **containment**.

Peaceful co-existence between the USSR and the USA was not possible.

The Soviet Union believed the West wanted to destroy communism.

The USA was more powerful than the Soviet Union and should lead the West in standing up to the Soviet Union.

The Long Telegram

In order to protect itself, the Soviet Union wanted to spread communism and destroy capitalism.

Only strong resistance would deter Soviet aggression. Peaceful negotiation was pointless.

Seven months after the Long Telegram, Novikov, the Soviet Ambassador to the USA, completed his assessment of US foreign policy. This telegram also had a major impact on US-Soviet relations because it further convinced Stalin that he needed to protect the Soviet Union from the USA by creating a buffer zone in Eastern Europe.

The USA was bent on world dominance.

The USA was not interested in cooperating with the USSR.

Eventually the USA planned on going to war with the Soviet Union in order to destroy it.

The Novikov Telegram

The USA was investing heavily in its military and setting up strategic bases around the world.

The USA wanted to remove Soviet influence from Eastern Europe and set up American-backed governments that would be hostile to the Soviet Union.

The development of the Cold War

The Truman Doctrine and the Marshall Plan, 1947

In the two years following the Second World War, the USA took little active role in European affairs. For them, it was mission complete: Nazi Germany had been defeated. In 1947, however, President Truman fundamentally changed US foreign policy and increased Cold War tensions with the Truman Doctrine and the Marshall Plan.

Stalin is in the process of taking over Eastern Europe.

Western Europe is in economic ruin, especially France and Italy.

The Italian and French communist parties are growing in support.

In Greece and Turkey, non-communist forces, backed by Britain, are fighting communist rebels.

Poverty encourages support of communist parties because they promise everyone a decent standard of living.

Britain has told me that it can no longer afford to support Greece and Turkey.

I believe that Stalin wants to spread communism around the world.

Truman's worries

The Truman Doctrine

On 12 March 1947, Truman delivered a speech to the US **Congress**. This would have an important impact on US-Soviet relations.

 STRETCHIT!

Full versions of Truman's 1947 speech to Congress are easy to find on the internet. It gives a vivid insight into the USA's hostile attitude to the Soviet Union.

Truman Doctrine	• Economic aid of $400 million to Greece and Turkey. • It was the duty of the USA to contain communism. • The USA would provide economic and military assistance to any country threatened with communist takeover.

Impact on US-Soviet relations	• The Greek and Turkish governments defeated the communist political parties, largely due to US economic aid. • Rivalry increased because Truman had publicly identified the Soviet Union as the number one threat to the USA. • The USA put itself forward as the leader of the fight against communism throughout the world. • The USA became far more involved in European affairs, which the USSR resented. • It led to the Marshall Plan, which hugely increased US-Soviet tension.

DO IT!

Do you think Marshall Aid should be seen as a generous gift to Europe from the USA? Make two lists, one listing the positive aspects of Marshall Aid and another listing the negative aspects.

The Marshall Plan

The Truman Doctrine stated the USA would use its economic power to help protect countries from communist takeover. **US Secretary of State**, General George Marshall explained that this meant that the USA would give money to help European countries recover from the Second World War. If people were no longer living in economic ruin and poverty, he argued, they would be much less likely to turn to communism.

Many in the US government were unwilling to support an expensive aid programme. Attitudes changed in February 1948 when the communists overthrew the government of Czechoslovakia. Soon after, the Marshall Plan, officially the European Recovery Program, became law.

STRETCH IT!

Use the internet to find examples of Soviet propaganda cartoons attacking the Marshall Plan. Consider how the Soviet's portray the Americans in these cartoons and the motives of Marshall Aid.

The Marshall Plan had a huge impact on US-Soviet relations, greatly increasing tension:

- The Soviets attacked the whole scheme as 'dollar **imperialism**'. They claimed the plan was no more than a US ploy to takeover the economies of Western Europe.

- It forbade Eastern European satellite states from taking part in the scheme.

- In response to the Marshall Plan, Stalin established Cominform and Comintern.

Marshall Aid: Factfile

- Between 1948 and 1952 over £13 billion of Marshall Aid was given to 16 Western European countries, including Britain, France and West Germany.
- It came in the form of food, fuel, industrial and agricultural machinery, technical advice and investment.
- It was distributed by the Organisation for European Economic Cooperation (OEEC).
- It greatly helped these countries rebuild and recover from the devastation of the Second World War.

The significance of Cominform and Comecon

Cominform The communist Information Bureau, established 1947	**Comecon** Council of Mutual Economic Assistance, established 1949
Membership USSR, all the satellite states and French and Italian communist parties	**Membership** USSR and all the satellite states
Function Stalin used Cominform to: • ensure that no satellite state accepted Marshall Aid • encourage protests and strikes in France and Italy against the Marshall Plan • ensure satellite states followed the same foreign and economic policies as the Soviet Union • spread propaganda attacking the West (e.g. comparing to Nazis) • Encourage obedience to the Soviet Union. In 1948 Yugoslavia was expelled from Cominform for being too independent.	**Function** Comecon was Stalin's version of the Marshall Plan but with little money available. It aimed to promote economic development by organising trade agreements between members. The Soviet Union used it to gain greater control over Eastern Europe's economies by: • securing access to cheap goods and raw materials for the USSR • discouraging satellite states from trading with the West • imposing over time, its economic model on the satellite states, including state ownership of factories and farms.

The Berlin Crisis

In 1945 Germany was divided into four zones and so was Berlin. The city was 100 miles inside the Soviet zone of Germany and linked to the west by road, rail and air routes.

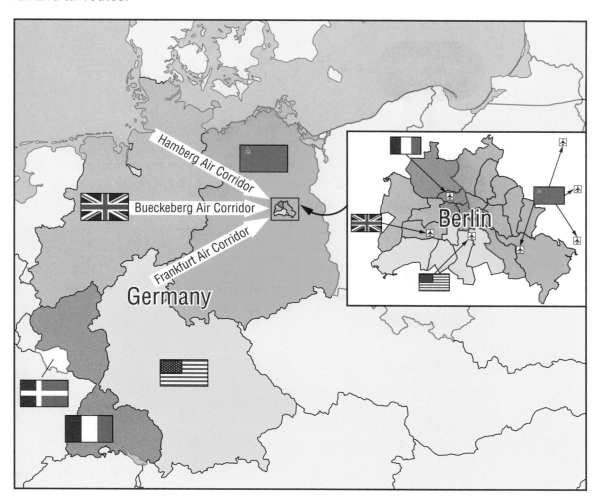

Causes of the Berlin Crisis

Conflicting policies on Germany

This crisis came about because the Soviet Union and the West had very different views about what should happen to post-war Germany.

The West's plan for Germany	The Soviet plan for Germany
• Democratic • Capitalist • Economically successful	• Communist • Economically weak • Paying large reparations to the Soviet Union
Advantage to the USA: Germany would no longer need large amounts of aid. It could become a valuable trading partner and Europe's first line of defence against the USSR.	Advantage to the Soviet Union: Germany would never threaten the Soviet Union again – security was Stalin's central concern. Reparations would help rebuild the Soviet Union.

1 Jot down one similarity and one difference between Cominform and Comecon.

2 Create a flow diagram explaining how the Cold War became colder following the introduction of the Truman Doctrine. Use the diagram to show how this led to the Marshall Plan, which in turn led to Cominform and Comecon.

2 The actions of the West

Stalin knew that the economic resources of the West outmatched his own. His great fear was that the West would end up uniting their zones and creating a powerful West Germany, which would eventually take over the communist eastern zone. These fears came to a head in 1948.

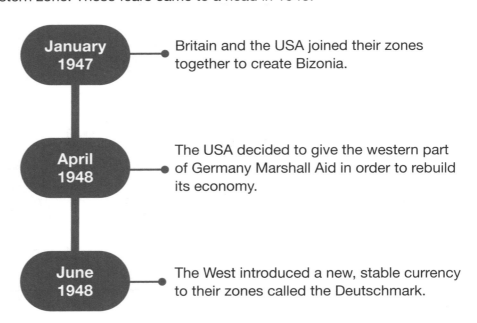

January 1947 — Britain and the USA joined their zones together to create Bizonia.

April 1948 — The USA decided to give the western part of Germany Marshall Aid in order to rebuild its economy.

June 1948 — The West introduced a new, stable currency to their zones called the Deutschmark.

The Berlin Blockade

Stalin decided to hit back at the West's weakest point in Germany – Berlin. On 24 June 1948 he cut all road, rail and canal routes into the city from the West. The blockade of Berlin had started. Stalin aimed to drive the West out and unite the city under communist rule.

NAILIT!

Students frequently mix up the Berlin Crisis and the building of the Berlin Wall. Make sure you read the exam question carefully and write about the correct event.

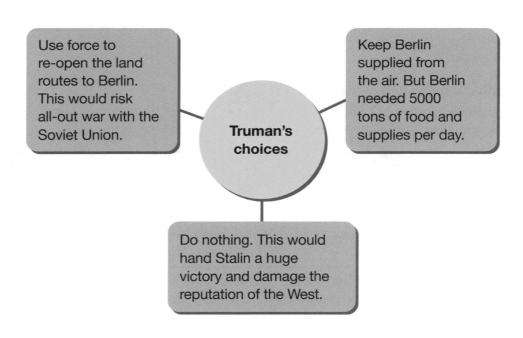

Use force to re-open the land routes to Berlin. This would risk all-out war with the Soviet Union.

Keep Berlin supplied from the air. But Berlin needed 5000 tons of food and supplies per day.

Truman's choices

Do nothing. This would hand Stalin a huge victory and damage the reputation of the West.

The Berlin Airlift

Truman did not want to fight a war, nor could he back down. As a result he decided to keep West Berlin supplied by air. The Berlin Airlift lasted for eleven months until Stalin admitted defeat and lifted the blockade in May 1949.

> ### The Berlin Airlift: Factfile
>
> - At the height of the operation, an allied aircraft carrying the food and fuel needed to keep the West Berliners going, landed in Berlin every minute.
> - The Soviets made life difficult for the Allied pilots by flying across the air corridors and placing weather balloons in awkward positions.
> - Stalin was not prepared to shoot any Allied planes down because he did not want to risk war.
> - The airlift cost the USA $350 million and Britain £17 million.

DOIT!

Do you think Truman made the right choice in settling on an airlift? Bullet point reasons for and against Truman's three options.

STRETCHIT!

The Berlin Blockade and airlift was extensively reported at the time. Use the internet to watch some of the British Pathé news reports.

The impact on international relations

The start of the Cold War	Permanent division of Germany	Formation of NATO
The Berlin Crisis was the first serious clash between East and West. It showed that the Grand Alliance was firmly over. The Soviet Union and the USA were now Cold War enemies.	Germany would remain divided for over 40 years. In May 1949 the western zones combined to form the Federal Republic of Germany (West Germany). In October 1949 the eastern zone became the German Democratic Republic (East Germany).	The West viewed the Berlin Crisis as the East becoming more aggressive. In order to protect themselves against the Soviet Union, 12 western nations (including the USA, Canada, France and Britain) signed a treaty setting up the North Atlantic Treaty Organisation (NATO) in April 1949. They agreed that if one member was attacked, others would come to its aid.

The significance of the formation of NATO

- Cold War tensions increased.
- The USA was now committed to playing a big role in the defence of Western Europe, which angered the Soviets.
- The USSR condemned NATO. It said it was an offensive alliance aimed at the Soviet Union and showed the West were preparing for war.
- In response, the Warsaw Pact was formed in 1955 (see page 24).

DOIT!

To summarise the Berlin Crisis, jot down three of its causes, three events and three impacts.

The Cold War intensifies

The Warsaw Pact

The Soviet Union saw NATO as an aggressive military alliance, which would one day invade the Soviet Union. This fear increased in 1955 because West Germany became a NATO member and started to rebuild its army.

In response, in 1955 the Soviet Union formed a defensive military alliance – the Warsaw Pact, with seven other communist countries: East Germany, Poland, Hungary, Czechoslovakia, Romania, Bulgaria and Albania. They agreed that if any member was attacked, the others would all help. A joint command structure was set up, which placed the armies of each member under a Soviet Supreme Commander.

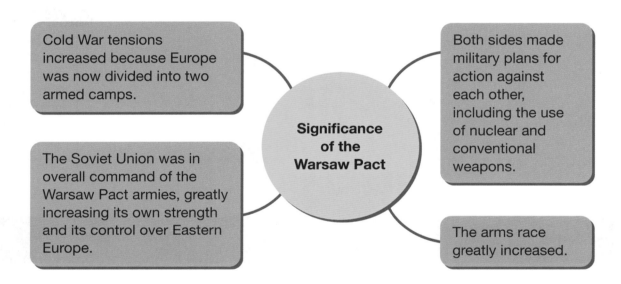

Cold War tensions increased because Europe was now divided into two armed camps.

The Soviet Union was in overall command of the Warsaw Pact armies, greatly increasing its own strength and its control over Eastern Europe.

Significance of the Warsaw Pact

Both sides made military plans for action against each other, including the use of nuclear and conventional weapons.

The arms race greatly increased.

The arms race

The nuclear arms race was one of the most alarming features of the Cold War superpower competition. During the 1950s both sides rapidly expanded their nuclear arsenals (see diagram on next page).

The space race was happening at the same time and was related to the arms race. In 1957 the Soviet Union launched *Sputnik*, a satellite that could orbit the Earth in 1.5 hours. The USA saw this as a real threat because it suggested they were falling behind Soviet technology. They also feared that the powerful rocket that put *Sputnik* into space could one day be used to launch nuclear missiles against the USA. In response, they increased spending on their own space and weapons programmes.

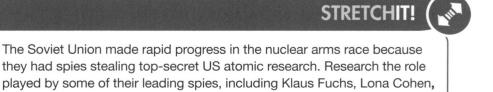

STRETCHIT!

The Soviet Union made rapid progress in the nuclear arms race because they had spies stealing top-secret US atomic research. Research the role played by some of their leading spies, including Klaus Fuchs, Lona Cohen, Julius and Ethel Rosenberg, and Rudolf Abel.

The back and forth nature of the arms race

The USA

> **July 1945** The USA tested its first nuclear weapon, codenamed 'Trinity', in New Mexico.
>
> **August 1945** The USA dropped atomic bombs on the Japanese cities of Hiroshima and Nagasaki, devastating the cities and killing around 200,000 unarmed civilians.

> **1952** The USA tested the next generation of nuclear weapons – the hydrogen bomb. The explosion was seven hundred times the force of the Hiroshima bomb.

> **1958** The USA successfully tested the Atlas missile – its own ICBM.

The USSR

> **1949** The Soviet Union detonated its first atomic weapon, codenamed 'First Lightning'.

> **1953** The USSR tested its own hydrogen bomb.
>
> **1957** The USSR successfully tested the world's first **ICBM** called the R-7. It flew for 3700 miles.

Significance of the arms race

- The arms race further increased rivalry and tension between the superpowers. Each side felt threatened so built more weapons, and then felt even more threatened.

- Ironically, it made war between the superpowers less likely. Under the theory of MAD (Mutually Assured Destruction) both sides realised a war would probably lead to the complete destruction of humanity. They were not prepared to risk this.

- Churchill described this situation as a 'balance of terror'. However, it didn't help to calm relations between the superpowers. Nor could either side afford to fall behind in the arms race.

- For the Soviet Union especially, the financial cost of the arms race was a huge burden. This would create problems for the USSR later in the Cold War.

DO IT!

Using 20 words maximum, record the key stages of the arms race between the USA and USSR.

The Hungarian Uprising

In 1956 the Hungarian people made a heroic attempt to gain their freedom from communist rule. The Soviet response was swift and brutal.

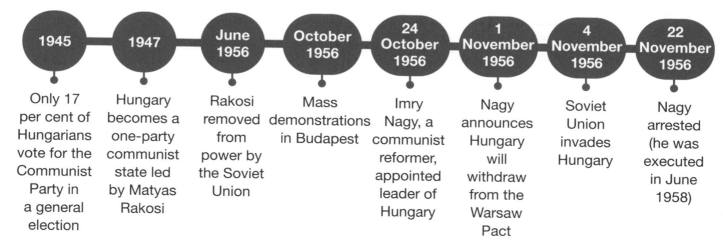

1945	1947	June 1956	October 1956	24 October 1956	1 November 1956	4 November 1956	22 November 1956
Only 17 per cent of Hungarians vote for the Communist Party in a general election	Hungary becomes a one-party communist state led by Matyas Rakosi	Rakosi removed from power by the Soviet Union	Mass demonstrations in Budapest	Imry Nagy, a communist reformer, appointed leader of Hungary	Nagy announces Hungary will withdraw from the Warsaw Pact	Soviet Union invades Hungary	Nagy arrested (he was executed in June 1958)

Causes of the uprising

1 **Hatred of communist rule**

Hungary had been under communist rule since 1948. This was deeply unpopular for a number of reasons:

- The Hungarian communist leader, Matyas Rakosi, used terror and violence to keep control. The Hungarian secret police (AVH) were particularly feared by ordinary people.

- Many Hungarians were Roman Catholic. They hated the way their religion was attacked. Priests, monks and nuns were persecuted and many arrested. Cardinal Mindszenty, the leader of the Hungarian Catholic Church, was imprisoned for life in 1949.

- The Soviet Union controlled the Hungarian economy through Comecon. They took food and industrial products without paying a fair price.

- Living standards gradually declined. In 1956 things worsened with poor harvests, bread and fuel shortages.

2 **De-Stalinisation**

In 1953 Stalin died. After a power struggle, Nikita Khrushchev emerged as leader of the Soviet Union. In February 1956 he made a major speech condemning Stalin for his use of terror. The Soviet Union, he said, needed a period of **de-Stalinisation**. Some Hungarians took Khrushchev's speech to mean that now was the time to push for the removal of their own hated leaders, many of whom had been put in place by Stalin.

Key events

In July 1956 large numbers of Hungarians took to the streets to demand an end to Rakosi's rule.	Khrushchev wanted to keep law and order in Hungary, so he replaced Rakosi with Erni Gero. The problem was Gero was also unpopular and so demonstrations continued.	On 23 October 1956 a mass demonstration took place in Budapest. A crowd pulled down a huge statue of Stalin. When the AVH began to fire on protestors, they were killed by the crowd.	On 24 October the Soviets agreed to appoint a more moderate, popular leader – Imry Nagy (pronounced Nodj). Nagy quickly announced sweeping reforms.

NAILIT!

Remembering people's names and how to spell them can be a tricky part of this topic. Make a list of all the names you come across and give yourself regular spelling tests to help you learn them.

Khrushchev's response

Khrushchev's priority was maintaining Soviet security and he could not allow a key Warsaw Pact member to leave. He also feared other Pact members would follow Hungary's example. On 4 November Soviet tanks moved into Budapest and after bitter fighting, the uprising was crushed.

- Over 2500 Hungarians were killed. 200,000 fled the country.

- Nagy was arrested and later executed after a secret trial.

- Cardinal Mindszenty spent the next 15 years hiding in the US embassy before he was allowed to leave Hungary.

- Hungary remained in the Warsaw Pact and under Soviet control.

- A loyal communist – Janos Kadar, was appointed Hungary's new leader.

> ### Nagy's reforms
>
> - Freedom of speech was introduced
> - Political parties could be formed
> - Democratic elections would be held
> - The AVH were disbanded
> - Cardinal Mindszenty was released from prison
> - All Soviet troops would have to leave Hungary
> - Hungary would leave the Warsaw Pact
> - It would become neutral in the Cold War

The international reaction to the Soviet invasion

1. The United Nations condemned the Soviet response but took no further action.

2. The Americans were angry at the brutal Soviet response and condemned Khrushchev. However, the USA did not provide Hungary with military aid because: it was too busy trying to sort out the Suez Crisis – the British and French invasion of Egypt; there was no easy way to get military aid to Hungary; in an age of nuclear weapons, it was too dangerous to intervene.

3. The USA's decision not to aid the rebels damaged its own international reputation. It had initially encouraged Hungarians to stand up to the Soviet Union. By not providing military support, many felt the USA had let the Hungarian people down.

Khrushchev therefore retained control of Hungary. He also sent a clear warning to the satellite states about the dangers of trying to break free from Soviet control.

STRETCHIT!

The renowned photojournalist Michael Rougier covered the Hungarian Uprising for *Life* magazine. Use the internet to find examples of the many striking photographs he took during his time in Budapest.

DOIT!

Display the results of the Hungarian Uprising in a different form. It could be a table, bullet point notes or even an annotated picture.

CHECKIT! ✓

1. Outline three reasons the Grand Alliance started to fall apart at the Potsdam Conference.

2. Describe Comecon, Stalin's answer to the Marshall Plan.

3. Explain two ways in which the Warsaw Pact increased Cold War tensions.

4. Why did the USA do so little to stop the Soviet invasion of Hungary?

Part Two:
Cold War crises 1958–70

NAIL IT!

Learn the key details of the East Germany refugee crisis. It was the major cause of increased tensions over Berlin.

Tensions over Berlin and the Berlin Wall

Khrushchev likened West Berlin to a fish bone stuck in his throat. He wanted to get the Western powers out of the city for good. Khrushchev failed in this aim, however, and this led to the construction of the Berlin Wall.

Increased tensions over Berlin

As a consequence of the Berlin Blockade, Germany was formally split into two countries in 1949. Berlin, now surrounded by East Germany, was itself divided between East and West. By the late 1950s this city was becoming a major source of Cold War tension for the following reasons.

DO IT!

Write a paragraph explaining why Khrushchev wanted the West out of Berlin.

1 Refugees. East German soldiers patrolled the border between East and West Germany and prevented anyone trying to flee the communist regime. However, huge numbers were still managing to escape through Berlin.

- Berlin was the one 'gap' in the Iron Curtain. East Germans just needed to travel into West Berlin, which was relatively easy. Once there, they could freely go to West Germany.

- The number of refugees leaving East Germany was enormous. By 1961 East Germany had lost one-sixth of its population. In 1961 20,000 people were leaving every month.

- This was highly embarrassing for the Soviets, who always claimed that communism was better than capitalism.

- The people leaving were mainly skilled workers and professionals, including engineers, doctors and teachers. Their loss was creating an economic crisis in East Germany.

STRETCH IT!

The Americans and British exploited the position of Berlin in order to spy on the Soviets. Investigate this further. You could look into the Teufelsberg spy station, as well Operation Gold, a top secret mission to tap into Soviet Army communications. Try and find out how successful they were.

Push factors in East Germany	Pull factors in the West
No political freedom	Political freedom
A repressive secret police called the **Stasi**	Higher living standards
Low living standards	Plentiful consumer goods
A shortage of basic goods	Higher wages

Living standards. During the 1950s East Germans could visit West Berlin and they liked what they saw: better housing and shops with plentiful goods. This was deliberate. The West had turned their half of the city into a show case for capitalism. The communist authorities were embarrassed because East Berlin was much poorer.

Intelligence gathering. The Soviets claimed that the West was using Berlin as a base to spy on its military.

Khrushchev's Berlin Ultimatum, 1958

The problems caused by Berlin created huge tension between East and West. In Khrushchev's view, the most effective solution was to get the Western powers out of the city.

In 1958 he issued an **ultimatum** which stated that all of Berlin belonged to East Germany and the West should leave within six months.

This demand sent shock waves through the West and significantly raised Cold War tensions. In order to try and resolve this crisis, a series of high level meetings were held, known as summits.

DO IT!

Take a picture of the table below to revise from later.

The summit meetings of 1959–61

Meeting	In attendance	Outcome
Geneva Summit, May 1959	US and Soviet Union foreign ministers	✗ No agreement on Berlin.
Camp David Summit, September 1959	Khrushchev and Eisenhower (their first meeting)	✗ No agreement on Berlin. ✓ Khrushchev agreed to withdraw his Ultimatum. ✓ It was decided to hold a follow up meeting.
Paris Summit, May 1960	Khrushchev and Eisenhower	✗ Shortly before this meeting, an American U2 spy plane was shot down over the Soviet Union. The talks collapsed when Eisenhower refused to apologise for this spy flight.
Vienna Summit, June 1961	Khrushchev and the newly elected US president, Kennedy	✗ Khrushchev believed Kennedy was inexperienced and could be bullied. ✗ He reissued the Berlin Ultimatum of 1958, demanding the West leave Berlin. ✗ Kennedy refused and shortly after increased US defence spending by over $3 billion.

STRETCH IT!

On 1 May 1960 a US U2 spy plane was shot down over the Soviet Union while taking photographs of military bases. The pilot, Gary Powers, parachuted to safety and was captured.

The construction of the Berlin Wall, 1961

DO IT!

Bullet point three details about the Berlin Wall.

By the end of the Vienna Summit, it was clear that Khrushchev was not going to remove the Western powers from Berlin. With the refugee crisis worsening, he decided on a radical course of action.

- In the early hours of 13 August 1961, the East German police used coils of barbed wire to seal off most of the crossing points between East and West Berlin.

- Over the next few weeks the barbed wire was replaced by a 27-mile concrete wall running through the city centre, separating East and West Berlin.

- The Wall was then extended around the whole of West Berlin, separating it from the rest of East Germany. In total it was 96 miles long.

- East German border guards had orders to shoot anyone trying to cross the Wall.

- Over time the East German authorities developed the Wall so it became almost impossible to escape.

- Eight official crossing points were established in the Wall. Foreign nationals and military personnel mainly used Checkpoint Charlie.

- West Berliners could apply for permits to cross into East Berlin. Only in rare circumstances were East Berliners permitted to cross the Wall.

The key features of the Berlin Wall in 1968

alarm fence

asphalt road

watchtower

the 'death strip'

animal fence

the wall itself

bunker

tank barriers

The impact of the Berlin Wall

For the people of Berlin, the Wall brought a great deal of sadness and anger. The escape route to the West was now closed. Families and friends were split apart. Between 1961 and 1989 approximately 140 people were killed trying to cross the Wall.

The impact on US-Soviet relations was mixed. In some ways it helped reduce tensions over Berlin but it also had serious negative consequences.

✓ The flow of refugees was stopped and the economic crisis in East Germany eased. A major source of tension was therefore resolved.

✓ By building the Wall, Khrushchev seemed to accept the presence of the West in Berlin. There was no repeat of his 1958 Ultimatum.

✓ Although the USA complained about the Wall, they did not try to take it down. It was not worth a war.

✗ It sparked a tense tank stand-off at Checkpoint Charlie (see below).

✗ In the West the Wall became a symbol of all that was wrong with communism. It showed that the Soviet Union had to effectively imprison the people of East Germany to stop them leaving.

✗ Khrushchev mistakenly concluded that Kennedy was a weak leader by allowing the Wall to be built. This encouraged him to challenge Kennedy again in Cuba (see page 33).

Tank stand-off at Checkpoint Charlie

- East German troops started checking the identity documents of American troops passing through Checkpoint Charlie.

- The Americans claimed this was a violation of the Yalta Agreement, which stated that Allied powers should have free movement throughout Berlin.

- On 27 October 1961 the USA stationed tanks on its side of Checkpoint Charlie in protest.

- The Soviets responded by positioning tanks on their side.

- For 16 hours tanks and soldiers faced each other. Many people thought war was imminent.

- Khrushchev and Kennedy cooperated to work out a diplomatic solution and the tanks were withdrawn.

Kennedy's visit to Berlin in 1963

Kennedy visited West Berlin in June 1963. He was greeted as a hero and made an inspirational speech. Kennedy stated that the people of Berlin were in the front line in the struggle against communism. He predicted a happier, peaceful future; in time the Wall would fall and Berlin would be reunited. He closed the speech by expressing solidarity, saying 'I am a citizen of Berlin'. This speech and Kennedy's visit was very significant:

It showed his support for the people of Berlin, both East and West.

The speech served as a powerful attack on the Soviet Union and the communist system.

It gave some hope to the people trapped in East Berlin.

It indicated that the USA had no intention of abandoning West Berlin to the Soviets.

US President Kennedy speaking in West Berlin, June 1963

DO IT!

Produce a revision page summarising the impact of the Berlin Wall. Describe its effect on East Germany and its mixed impact on superpower relations.

The Cuban Revolution and the Cuban Missile Crisis

Cuba became part of the Cold War following a socialist revolution in 1959. Three years later the Cuban Missile Crisis saw a tense 13-day confrontation between the USA and the Soviet Union when nuclear war seemed a real possibility.

The Cuban Revolution and US-Cuban relations

In January 1959 revolution hit Cuba. Fidel Castro, a **left-wing** rebel, seized power from the unpopular and repressive military dictator, General Batista. Initially the USA recognised Castro's new government, but US-Cuban relations soon deteriorated. In 1960 the USA stopped all aid to Cuba and imposed a **trade embargo**. This threatened to bankrupt the Cuban economy, which largely depended on selling sugar to the USA. Then in January 1961, the USA broke off all diplomatic links with Cuba and closed its embassy in Havana. Castro was no longer seen by the USA as the legitimate leader of Cuba.

STRETCH IT!

To see how Castro was initially viewed as a romantic hero by many Americans, use the internet to search out the 1959 Ed Sullivan interview with Castro.

Reasons for the decline in US-Cuban relations

The US government disliked Castro because he was left-wing and anti-American.

The Americans did not want a left-wing country in their 'backyard'. Cuba was located just 90 miles off the coast of Florida.

Castro started establishing close relations with the Soviet Union.

Castro **nationalised** all American-owned companies and refused to pay compensation.

Soviet relations with Cuba

The US trade embargo helped push Cuba towards the Soviets, as Castro asked the Soviet Union to help avert economic disaster. Khrushchev was keen to gain an ally so close to the USA and readily agreed to purchase Cuban sugar.

DO IT!

Note down three reasons why Cuba became an ally of the Soviet Union rather than the United States.

STRETCH IT!

In December 1962 Cuba was given $53 million worth of food and medicine by the US government to secure the release of the 1100 rebels taken prisoner following the failed Bay of Pigs invasion.

The Bay of Pigs incident, 1961

The USA was not prepared to see Cuba become a Soviet outpost. In April 1961 President Kennedy gave the go ahead for a **CIA**-backed invasion of the island and 1400 anti-Castro Cubans landed at the Bay of Pigs. The CIA hoped this would spark a general uprising against Castro, leading to his removal. However, the invasion was a disaster. Within three days all the rebels had been captured or killed.

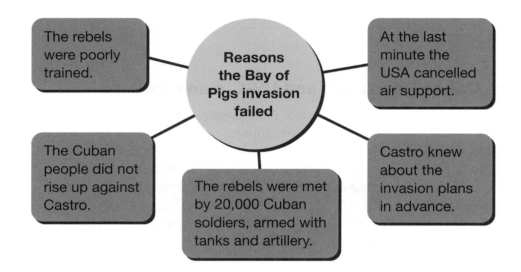

The significance of the Bay of Pigs incident

- Kennedy was humiliated. He was made to look weak and inexperienced in foreign policy matters.

- Kennedy approved Operation Mongoose, a secret CIA programme to remove Castro from power using underhand means such as assassination.

- Castro's position in Cuba was strengthened. He became a national hero for defeating a foreign-backed invasion.

- It ended all chances of a friendly US-Cuban relationship.

- It strengthened Soviet-Cuban relations. Castro announced that he was a communist and asked Khrushchev to help defend Cuba.

- The Soviet Union started supplying Cuba with weapons to help defend the island against further American attack. This would lead to the Cuban Missile Crisis (see below).

DO IT!

Write a paragraph explaining why the Bay of Pigs incident achieved the reverse of what Kennedy wanted.

The Cuban Missile Crisis

In early 1962 Khrushchev and Castro agreed to install Soviet nuclear missiles on Cuba.

- This would stop the USA from invading Cuba.

- It would solve a strategic weakness. The USA had placed **Jupiter missiles** in Turkey, very close to the Soviet Union's southern border. However, the Soviet Union had no similar military bases close to the USA.

By summer, construction on the missile bases in Cuba had started.

Key events of the Cuban Missile Crisis, 1962

14 October — An American U2 spy plane discovered intermediate range missile sites under construction on Cuba. A further spy plane discovered 20 Soviet ships in the Atlantic Ocean, heading for Cuba. These were carrying nuclear missiles.

15 October — Kennedy was informed about the missile sites. He was told that once they became operational, most of the USA would be within their range. The crisis had started.

16 October — Kennedy called an emergency meeting with his military and political advisers. This group was known as the Executive Committee (Excomm). For the next few days they discussed how to respond. The preferred options were either 1) air strikes against the missile sites or 2) a naval blockade to stop the missiles arriving in Cuba.

US military preparations

- More than 100,000 troops were sent to Florida to prepare for an invasion of Cuba.
- Four air squadrons were readied for air strikes.
- B-52 bombers loaded with nuclear weapons were in the air at all times.
- 145 intercontinental ballistic missiles were prepared for immediate firing.

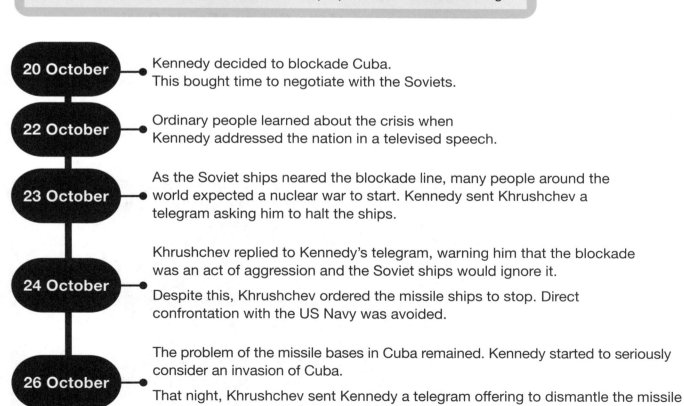

20 October — Kennedy decided to blockade Cuba.
This bought time to negotiate with the Soviets.

22 October — Ordinary people learned about the crisis when Kennedy addressed the nation in a televised speech.

23 October — As the Soviet ships neared the blockade line, many people around the world expected a nuclear war to start. Kennedy sent Khrushchev a telegram asking him to halt the ships.

24 October — Khrushchev replied to Kennedy's telegram, warning him that the blockade was an act of aggression and the Soviet ships would ignore it.

Despite this, Khrushchev ordered the missile ships to stop. Direct confrontation with the US Navy was avoided.

26 October — The problem of the missile bases in Cuba remained. Kennedy started to seriously consider an invasion of Cuba.

That night, Khrushchev sent Kennedy a telegram offering to dismantle the missile sites if the blockade was lifted and the USA promised not to invade Cuba.

DOIT!

1 Create your own calendar of the Cuban Missile Crisis. Pick out five key events to remember.

2 On which day do you think the crisis was at its worst and why? When do you think Kennedy knew that he would not need to go to war with the USSR?

27 October Khrushchev sent a second, more aggressive telegram to Kennedy demanding the dismantling of the US missile sites in Turkey.

A U2 spy plane was shot down over Cuba, but Kennedy refused to take action.

That night, Robert Kennedy met secretly with the Soviet ambassador and offered the USSR a deal.

28 October Khrushchev agreed to the proposal and the crisis was over.

The USA will:
- end the blockade
- promise never to invade Cuba
- dismantle the missile bases in Turkey (but this must be kept a secret).

The USSR will:
- dismantle the missile bases in Cuba.

Robert Kennedy

NAILIT!

As well as learning specific facts about Cuba, keep the big picture in mind for narrative style questions. Make sure you know how the Cuban Revolution, Bay of Pigs incident and the Cuban Missile Crisis all link together.

STRETCHIT!

Robert Kennedy, younger brother of the President, played a key role in the Cuban Missile Crisis. He was the US Attorney General, in charge of providing the government with legal advice.

The consequences of the Cuban Missile Crisis

✓ Cuba was protected from any future US invasion. The communist system survives to this day.

✓ Jupiter missiles were removed from Turkey.

✗ The deal was kept secret so Khrushchev gained no credit for it.

✗ Many in the Soviet Communist Party did not like the way Khrushchev had backed down in the crisis. They claimed he made the Soviet Union look weak.

✗ Partly because of this criticism, Khrushchev was removed as leader in 1964. He was replaced by Leonid Brezhnev.

✓ In the West, Kennedy was widely praised as a great statesman. He had stood up to Khrushchev, forcing him to back down.

✓ All Soviet missiles were withdrawn from Cuba.

✗ Cuba remained a communist nation, despite being in America's 'backyard'.

✗ Behind the scenes, many of America's allies were annoyed with Kennedy because he did not consult them during the crisis.

Positive (✓) and negative (✗) consequences of the Cuban Missile Crisis for Khrushchev and Kennedy

Both sides were scared by how close they had come to nuclear war. As a result, there was a move to improve relations and this resulted in several key agreements.

The Outer Space Treaty, 1967: Both sides agreed not to place nuclear weapons in orbit around the Earth, on the moon or anywhere in space. Space would only be used for peaceful purposes.

The Nuclear Non-Proliferation Treaty, 1968: This was designed to prevent the spread of nuclear weapons. The USA, Soviet Union and Britain – all states with nuclear weapons – promised never to share their nuclear weapon's technology. Many other non-nuclear states also joined the Treaty, promising never to develop nuclear weapons.

Consequences of the Cuban Missile Crisis

The Hotline Agreement, 1963: Communication between each side during the Cuban Missile Crisis was very slow – it often took six hours for messages to be sent and received. It was realised that fast communication would be key to solving any further crises. As a result a special teleprinter system was established in the **Kremlin** and **Pentagon**, allowing messages to be sent and received much more rapidly.

The Limited Test Ban Treaty, 1963: This treaty banned the testing of nuclear weapons in the atmosphere, in outer space and under water. This reflected growing concern about nuclear **fall out**. The Treaty had actually been under discussion for eight years – the more constructive atmosphere following the Cuban Missile Crisis was important in getting it agreed.

DO IT!

1 Take a picture of the spider diagram above. For each consequence, try and recall two facts. Then write four catchy headlines to sum up the four main consequences of the Cuban Missile Crisis.

2 Create a one-page revision summary of the Cuban Missile Crisis. Divide your page into three columns: Causes, Main events, and Consequences.

STRETCH IT!

The first message transmitted over the hotline was 'The quick brown fox jumped over the lazy dog's back 1234567890'. Can you work out why?

Czechoslovakia and the Prague Spring

In 1948 the Communist Party seized power in Czechoslovakia and established a hard-line regime, closely tied to the Soviet Union. Twenty years later Alexander Dubček, a communist leader with a fresh outlook, made a doomed attempt to reform this system.

Opposition to Soviet control

- The Czechoslovakian leader, Antonin Novotny, was widely hated. He was a hard-line communist who resisted calls to reform his strict regime.

- There was no freedom of speech and the press, radio and television were heavily censored. Before the war Czechoslovakia had been a democracy, making this particularly hard to bear.

- The secret police, known as State Security or StB, were feared. They tapped telephones, read people's mail and arrested anyone who spoke out.

- There were few consumer goods and living standards had been steadily falling following an economic downturn in the early 1960s. Novotny's efforts to improve the economy were unsuccessful.

The Prague Spring

In early 1968 Novotny lost the support of the Soviet leader Brezhnev and stepped down as leader. He was replaced by Dubček; a committed communist with a belief that the political system needed to make people happy. As a result, he announced a sweeping programme of reforms.

Dubček believed in 'socialism with a human face' and his reforms created genuine excitement among many ordinary people. For the first time since 1948 people were able to talk openly about politics. This move towards democracy was known as the 'Prague Spring'.

STRETCH IT!

During the Nazi occupation of Czechoslovakia, Novotny worked for the communist underground movement. In 1941 he was arrested by the Nazi secret police and sent to Mauthausen concentration camp, where he stayed until liberated by American troops in 1945.

Dubček's reforms

- Freedom of speech
- **Freedom of assembly**
- The end of press censorship
- The release of all political prisoners
- A reduction in state control of the economy
- Limits on the powers of the secret police
- Easier travel to Western countries
- More power to regional governments
- A ten-year programme of political change, leading to democratic elections

The re-establishment of Soviet control

Learning from the experience of Hungary in 1956, Dubček was careful to assure the Soviet Union that he had no intention of leaving the Warsaw Pact. However, Brezhnev remained deeply suspicious about the Prague Spring for a number of reasons.

Brezhnev's fears over the Prague Spring

Other Eastern Bloc countries will want to implement similar reforms. This would endanger the stability of the Warsaw Pact and with it the Soviet Union's security.

Czechoslovakia might end up leaving the Warsaw Pact.

These changes will weaken the Communist Party's control over Czechoslovakia.

The hard-line leaders of Poland and East Germany also put pressure on Brezhnev to take firm action against Dubček. Initially, Brezhnev tried to slow down the pace of the Prague Spring through negotiation and pressure.

- In July 1968 Brezhnev met with Dubček to express his concerns.

- In early August a further meeting was held between Dubček and representatives from the USSR, Hungary, Poland, Bulgaria and East Germany.

- At the same time, Warsaw Pact troops performed very public military exercises close to the Czech border.

When these methods failed to produce the desired change, Brezhnev gave orders for the invasion of Czechoslovakia. On the night of 20 August 1968, 250,000 troops and 2000 tanks from five Warsaw Pact countries (the Soviet Union, Poland, Bulgaria, East Germany and Hungary) crossed the border into Czechoslovakia. The invasion, codenamed 'Operation Danube', was well planned and executed. Very soon the whole country was under total Soviet control. Dubček was arrested and taken to Moscow, where he was forced to sign an agreement ending most of his reforms.

 STRETCHIT!

Soviet command only used a small number of East German troops, for fear of reviving memories of the Nazi invasion of 1938.

Warsaw Pact tanks in
Prague, 1968

STRETCH IT!

Starting in the early hours of the invasion, a stream of huge Antonov AN-12 transport planes flew an entire airborne division into Prague Airport, complete with light tanks and artillery. Prague was rapidly captured as a result. Similar operations took place in other major cities.

The Brezhnev Doctrine

In the aftermath of the invasion, Brezhnev outlined a new hard-line foreign policy to ensure the Prague Spring could never be repeated. This became known in the West as the Brezhnev Doctrine. It stated the Soviet Union had the right to invade any country in Eastern Europe if they threatened the security of the whole Eastern Bloc.

In effect, this made it impossible for any Eastern Europe nation to:

1 Relax the strict communist system imposed by the Soviet Union.

2 Leave the Warsaw Pact.

This was an admission that countries would only stay communist if the USSR forced them to do so.

NAIL IT!

Make sure you know about the Brezhnev Doctrine. Do NOT get confused with any of the other 'doctrines' – the Truman, Reagan or Sinatra doctrines.

How Czechoslovakians responded to the Soviet invasion

A small number of Czechoslovakians attempted to fight back. In Prague barricades were set up in the streets and home-made bombs were thrown at tanks. However, Dubček told the people not to fight; there was no point. Instead, opposition was expressed non-violently.

Protesting in Prague's main square

Questioning Warsaw Pact soldiers about why they invaded

Fleeing the country

Non-violent methods of resisting the Soviet invasion

Giving wrong directions to soldiers

Placing flowers in the barrels of soldier's rifles

Anti-invasion graffiti

In April 1969 the Soviet Union replaced Dubček as leader with a hardliner, Gustáv Husák. He clamped down on opposition. In a process called 'normalisation' he also reversed Dubček's reforms. For the next 20 years, Czechoslovakia was a loyal Soviet ally. Dubček, meanwhile, was given a job in the Forestry Service.

International reaction

The reaction of the communist world

The Warsaw Pact invasion split the communist world.

- Hard-line governments such as Poland and East Germany were clearly supportive.
- Romania, a member of the Warsaw Pact, refused to send troops to join the invasion and its leader, Ceausescu, made a speech attacking Soviet policy.
- Albania withdrew from the Warsaw Pact in opposition.
- The Yugoslav and Chinese communist governments condemned the invasion.
- The communist parties of Western Europe were appalled by the invasion and distanced themselves from the Soviet Union.

The reaction of the West

Western governments all expressed outrage at the suppression of the Prague Spring. US-Soviet relations took a downturn. It confirmed the American view that the people of Eastern Europe were oppressed by the Soviet Union. President Johnson condemned the invasion and called for the withdrawal of all Warsaw Pact troops, but the USA offered no military assistance because:

- the Soviets had acted in their own sphere of influence
- the death toll from the invasion was relatively small
- the USA was too preoccupied fighting the Vietnam War.

STRETCH IT!

In January 1969 a young student named Jan Palach set fire to himself in Prague's main square, to protest at the Soviet invasion.

DO IT!

1 Create a revision page on the Prague Spring using only one side of A4. Divide it into three columns: Causes, Main events, and Outcomes.

2 Look back to the Hungarian Uprising (pages 25–27). Note down three similarities between the Hungarian Uprising and the Prague Spring and three differences.

CHECK IT!

1 Why did so many East Germans flee to West Germany in the 1950s?

2 Why should the 1961 Vienna Summit be regarded as a failure?

3 Describe the deal reached between Khrushchev and Kennedy to solve the Cuban Missile Crisis.

4 In what ways did the Soviet invasion of Czechoslovakia weaken Brezhnev's control over Eastern Europe?

Part Three:
The end of the Cold War 1970–91

STRETCHIT!

From the 1950s until mid 1970s, the United States fought a costly, and unsuccessful, war in Vietnam to try to protect capitalist South Vietnam from a communist takeover.

Attempts to reduce tension between East and West

Détente in the 1970s

Throughout the 1970s the USA and Soviet Union tried to reduce Cold War tensions. This became known as détente – a French word meaning 'release from tension'.

Reasons for détente

- Both sides were shocked at how close they had come to nuclear war during the Cuban Missile Crisis. This showed the dangers of not cooperating.

- The Soviet Union was spending huge amounts on defence – around 20 per cent of its budget. This money was desperately needed to improve living conditions at home.

- The United States was experiencing very little economic growth and wanted to spend less on expensive nuclear weapons.

- The United States was bogged down fighting the communists in the Vietnam War. To negotiate an end to this war, it needed the help of the Soviet Union.

- The Soviet Union had begun to argue with communist China. This meant that it wanted friendlier relations with the USA.

DOIT!

1 Why did both the USA and the Soviet Union want to pursue détente? Make a note of two reasons.

2 Bullet point three things agreed under SALT 1.

SALT 1

The first Strategic Arms Limitation Talks (SALT) began in November 1969. After difficult and complex negotiations, in May 1972 President Nixon and **General Secretary** Brezhnev agreed three separate deals.

The Anti-Ballistic Missile Treaty: Both sides were limited to two ABM sites, armed with 100 missile interceptors each. The idea was to ensure that each superpower remained vulnerable to the other's nuclear weapons, therefore deterring either side from launching an attack.

The Interim Treaty: A five-year freeze on the number of:

- ICMB **launchers**

- **SLBM** launchers

- submarines capable of carrying nuclear missiles.

The Basic Principles Agreement: Each side pledged to avoid confrontations that could lead to nuclear war.

A huge Titan II Intercontinental Ballistic Missile (ICBM) in its launching silo. The largest and heaviest missile built by the USA, it was in use from 1963–87.

The significance of SALT 1

✓ Both sides hailed the SALT 1 agreements as a huge achievement.

✓ Placing limits on nuclear weapon launchers slowed the arms race.

✓ It led to further talks on limiting nuclear weapons, called SALT 2.

✗ This treaty did not cut the huge number of nuclear weapons in existence, or even reduce the number of launchers.

✗ Strategic bombers, capable of dropping nuclear bombs, were not limited.

✗ No limits were placed on **MIRVs**, leaving both sides free to enlarge their nuclear arsenals by putting multiple nuclear weapons on each missile.

Helsinki Agreement

In 1975 the United States and Soviet Union, together with 33 other NATO and Warsaw Pact countries, signed a major diplomatic agreement. It consisted of three parts, referred to as 'baskets'.

The three baskets of the Helsinki Agreement

1 The existing borders between European countries could not be changed.

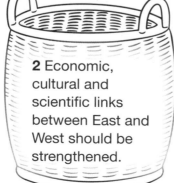

2 Economic, cultural and scientific links between East and West should be strengthened.

3 Human rights and freedoms had to be respected.

DO IT!

Create a balance sheet for SALT 1, with positives on one side and negatives on the other. Overall, do you think SALT 1 should be seen as a success?

STRETCHIT!

SALT 1 limited the United States to a maximum of 44 modern ballistic missile submarines and the Soviet Union to 62. This meant that both sides still had huge nuclear arsenals hidden under the oceans.

STRETCHIT!

As a symbol of détente, the first joint US-Soviet space mission took place in July 1975. An American Apollo spacecraft linked up with the Soviet Soyuz capsule. This led to the famous 'handshake in space' between cosmonaut Alexey Leonov and astronaut Tom Stafford, an event televised globally.

The significance of the Helsinki Agreement

✓ It demonstrated that the two sides could reach agreement on important matters.

✓ The West was delighted that the Soviet Union had agreed to uphold democratic rights such as freedom of thought, speech, religion and freedom from unfair arrest.

✓ Human rights' activists set up Helsinki Monitoring Groups in the Soviet Union and Eastern Europe. They tracked violations of the agreement, and highlighted these to the international community.

✗ The Soviet Union generally ignored the human rights' agreement and continued to imprison dissidents.

✗ By agreeing to existing European borders, it seemed as though the USA accepted the Soviet **annexation** of Estonia, Latvia and Lithuania, which occurred in 1940.

SALT 2

In 1972 the USA and the Soviet Union started further talks on arms control, known as SALT 2. The aim was to replace the Interim SALT 1 Treaty with something more far reaching. The negotiations were concluded in June 1979, when Soviet leader Brezhnev and President Jimmy Carter signed the SALT 2 Treaty.

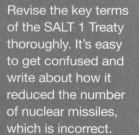

Create a revision spider diagram about détente in the 1970s. Cover the causes of détente as well as its main achievements: Salt 1, the Helsinki Agreement and Salt 2.

SALT 2 agreements: FactFile

- Each side LIMITED to 2400 launchers of all types.
- By 1981 the number of launches per side to be CUT to 2250.
- MIRV missiles LIMITED to 1320 per side.
- Construction of new land-based ICBM launchers BANNED.
- Development and testing of new missile programmes and new launching systems BANNED.

SALT 2 was a major breakthrough and promised to put a stop to the arms race. However, in December 1979 the Soviet Union invaded Afghanistan. In the new hostile atmosphere that followed, SALT 2 was never ratified (approved) by the US government.

NAILIT!

Revise the key terms of the SALT 1 Treaty thoroughly. It's easy to get confused and write about how it reduced the number of nuclear missiles, which is incorrect.

The mighty 155-metre-long Soviet Delta III class submarine, in service from 1976. It could carry 16 SLBMs, stored in the raised section of the hull.

Gorbachev's changing attitude

In 1982 Brezhnev (aged 75) died after 18 years in power. By 1985 power had passed to Mikhail Gorbachev, a much younger politician, with a more flexible, open-minded outlook. Unlike Brezhnev, Gorbachev realised that the Soviet Union had huge problems. If it was going to survive, these needed to be tackled.

The military budget was out of control.

The unpopular war in Afghanistan could not be won and was hugely expensive.

The quality of consumer goods was very poor.

Major problems in the Soviet Union

Industrial production was falling.

There were high levels of corruption within the Communist Party.

The standard of living was very low.

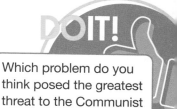

STRETCHIT!

In the early 1980s Soviet leadership was in crisis. Brezhnev's successor, Andropov, died 18 months after taking office, aged 69. His replacement, Chernenko, was already ill and lasted only a year before dying aged 73.

DOIT!

Which problem do you think posed the greatest threat to the Communist Party and why?

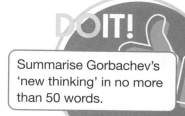

DOIT!

Summarise Gorbachev's 'new thinking' in no more than 50 words.

Gorbachev's 'new thinking'

Gorbachev was a committed communist and his aim was to save the Soviet Union, not destroy it. In order to tackle the country's huge problems, Gorbachev proposed the following ideas:

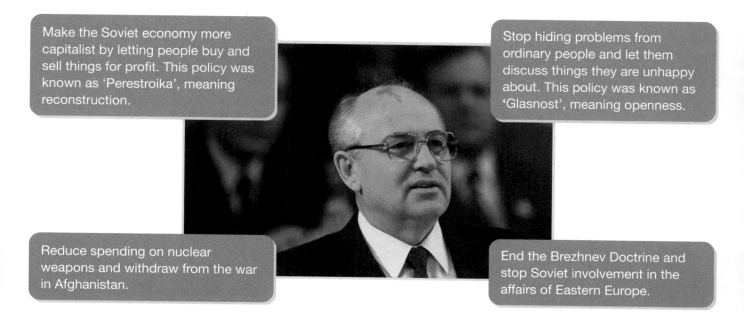

Make the Soviet economy more capitalist by letting people buy and sell things for profit. This policy was known as 'Perestroika', meaning reconstruction.

Stop hiding problems from ordinary people and let them discuss things they are unhappy about. This policy was known as 'Glasnost', meaning openness.

Reduce spending on nuclear weapons and withdraw from the war in Afghanistan.

End the Brezhnev Doctrine and stop Soviet involvement in the affairs of Eastern Europe.

Reagan's changing attitude

Gorbachev was not the only one with fresh thinking. By 1985 US President Reagan had begun to revise his hostile attitude towards the Soviet Union (see pages 48–49). He became more open and less aggressive because:

- He realised that Gorbachev did not want to expand communism around the world.

- He liked Gorbachev's reforms, especially the increasing freedoms from Glasnost.

- Gorbachev was a politician he could work with successfully.

The Intermediate-Range Nuclear Force (INF) Treaty

Reagan and Gorbachev met for the first time at the 1985 Geneva Summit. Both sides discussed how to cut the number of nuclear weapons. Although nothing was agreed, they established a good working relationship. A follow up meeting was held in Reykjavik in 1986, but the talks were unsuccessful because of fundamental disagreements about the US Strategic Defence Initiative (see page 49).

Success was finally achieved at the 1987 Washington Summit. Both sides signed the Intermediate Range Nuclear Force Treaty (INF) agreeing to abolish all land-based missiles with a range of 500 to 5500km.

Significance of the INF Treaty

✓ This was the first time the superpowers had agreed to eliminate an entire category of nuclear weapons.

✓ By 1991, 2692 US and Soviet nuclear missiles had been destroyed under this Treaty.

✓ Further arms control talks were held. In 1991 Gorbachev and US President George Bush signed the Strategic Arms Reduction Treaty I (START I). They agreed to destroy about one-third of their nuclear weapons.

✓ The arms race was ended.

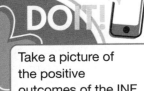

DO IT!

Take a picture of the positive outcomes of the INF Treaty (right) to look at while on the move.

STRETCHIT!

By the early 1980s intermediate range nuclear weapons were a growing source of tension. The Soviets **deployed** SS-20 missiles, capable of hitting Western Europe, in multiple locations throughout the Soviet Union. The Americans had placed Pershing II missiles in West Germany, directed at the Soviet Union.

Flashpoints

The significance of the Soviet invasion of Afghanistan

The period 1979–84 saw a number of Cold War flashpoints. These were dramatic increases in superpower tension. The first flashpoint was sparked by the Soviet invasion of Afghanistan. The significance of this stretched well beyond inflaming US hostility. It caused serious harm to Afghanistan and weakened communism in the Soviet Union.

In 1979 Afghanistan became very unstable. Radical Muslim fighters known as the *mujahideen* attacked the Afghan government, which was both non-Muslim and pro-Soviet. This developing civil war worried the Soviet leader, Brezhnev:

- He did not want to see a neighbouring ally collapse.

- He did not want Islamic fundamentalism spreading to the Muslim populations of the Soviet Union, located mainly in the south of the country near to Afghanistan.

To protect the interests of the Soviet Union, Brezhnev ordered an invasion of Afghanistan in December 1979. The resultant war against the *mujahideen* lasted until 1989, when the defeated Soviets withdrew.

Impact on the Soviet Union	Impact on Afghanistan
- 20,000 Soviet troops were killed. - The war cost $8 billion per year. - The invincible image of the Red Army was undermined. - The war was deeply unpopular in the Soviet Union.	- Approximately one million Afghans died. - One third of the country's population fled to Iran and Pakistan as refugees. - A bitter civil war developed between rival *mujahideen* groups following the Soviet departure.

The USA's reaction to the invasion

- The USA's focus on détente came to an end.

- Carter was worried in case the invasion of Afghanistan was the Soviet Union's first move in an attempt to gain control of the oil-rich Persian Gulf. He said the USA would use military force to protect its interests in this region. He also promised military aid to all the countries bordering Afghanistan. This became known as the Carter Doctrine.

- Carter asked the CIA to secretly provide the *mujahideen* with weapons and funding.

- The USA imposed **economic sanctions** on the Soviet Union, including banning exports of grain and advanced computer technology.

- Carter asked the US Senate not to ratify (agree to) the SALT 2 Treaty, and it never became official government policy.

 STRETCHIT!

Operation Cyclone was the code name for the CIA programme to arm and finance the *mujahideen* in Afghanistan from 1979 to 1989. It was the longest and most expensive CIA operation ever.

STRETCHIT!

Go online and look at the medal tables for the 1980 and 1984 Olympics. Which countries came out on top? Which countries were not represented?

The Olympic boycotts

As a result of the Soviet invasion of Afghanistan, the USA decided to boycott the 1980 Moscow Summer Olympics. In total, 65 countries joined the boycott including West Germany and Japan. This was a significant blow to the prestige of the Soviet Union, who had hoped to use the games to showcase communist achievements to the world.

In protest, the Soviet Union boycotted the 1984 Los Angeles Summer Olympics. It was joined by 14 allies, including all the East European satellite states. The boycotting countries organised their own sporting event, called the Friendship Games.

DOIT!

Name three ways the Soviet invasion of Afghanistan made the Cold War worse.

NAILIT!

You need to know about the significance of some key Cold War events including Cominform, Comecon, NATO, the arms race, the Warsaw Pact, the Bay of Pigs incident, Reagan and Gorbachev's changing attitudes, the invasion of Afghanistan, the fall of the Berlin Wall and the end of the Warsaw Pact. For significance, think: Why was this event important? What changes did it cause?

Reagan and the 'Second Cold War'

In 1981 Reagan became President of the United States. He was a fierce anti-communist and described the Soviet Union as an 'evil empire'. Reagan saw it as his mission to destroy communism. As a result he restarted the Cold War by massively increasing defence spending. He also aided the opponents of communism around the world.

Defence spending

Reagan increased the United States' defence budget by a huge $32 billion. He called this policy 'Peace through Strength'. The USSR would not risk threatening a much stronger USA.

Reagan's defence projects

Pershing and Cruise intermediate range nuclear missiles were stationed in Europe.

New Trident-class submarines were built, each one capable of carrying 24 nuclear missiles.

Neutron bomb production started. This bomb killed people but left infrastructure intact.

More B1 supersonic heavy bombers were built, designed to carry nuclear bombs to targets inside the Soviet Union.

New 'Peacekeeper' missiles were introduced. Each one carried ten nuclear warheads, making it the USA's most deadly weapon.

The Reagan Doctrine

As well as building up US military power, Reagan wanted to confront and even 'roll back' communism around the world. He therefore came up with the Reagan Doctrine: the USA would aid any country or group that opposed communism.

Reagan Doctrine: FactFile

- Stinger missiles, capable of shooting down aircraft, were sent to the *mujaheddin* in Afghanistan.
- Weapons and money were given to the Contras in Nicaragua. The Contras were a **right-wing** group fighting the country's left-wing government.
- Secret support was given to Solidarity (a **trade union**) in Poland.

The Strategic Defence Initiative (SDI)

In 1983 Reagan announced the most ambitious military project yet. Nicknamed 'Star Wars' by the press after the popular film, its real name was the Strategic Defence Initiative or SDI. This was a plan to place satellites in space armed with lasers. These would be able to shoot down Soviet nuclear missiles before they reached the USA.

The impact on the Cold War was huge. The Soviet Union demanded the USA abandon SDI. This was because it threatened the principle of MAD (Mutually Assured Destruction; see page 25) and so made a nuclear war more likely. The 1986 summit meeting in Reykjavik collapsed because of the fundamental differences between the two sides over SDI.

Ultimately, SDI forced Gorbachev to seek an end to the arms race because he knew the Soviet Union could not compete with this project. The Soviet economy was struggling and could not afford the huge cost of developing its own version of SDI. The Soviet Union also lacked the necessary computer technology. As a result, in 1987 Gorbachev dropped his objections to SDI and signed the INF Treaty (see page 46).

DO IT!

Create a one-page revision poster summarising all the ways that Reagan restarted the Cold War.

STRETCHIT!

In reality the USA did not have the technology to make the SDI a real possibility, but the Soviet Union did not know this.

The collapse of Soviet control of Eastern Europe

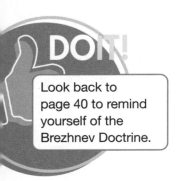

DO IT!

Look back to page 40 to remind yourself of the Brezhnev Doctrine.

The impact of Gorbachev's 'new thinking' on Eastern Europe

Gorbachev's new thinking led to the complete collapse of communist control in Eastern Europe, although this had not been his intention.

Food shortages

Lack of consumer goods

Problems in Eastern Europe

No democratic rights

Repressive governments

STRETCH IT!

Supporting the satellite states was expensive. The USSR spent approximately $40 billion annually on communist governments around the world. Gorbachev wanted to use this money for domestic reform.

Eastern Europe suffered many of the same problems as the Soviet Union itself. In order to keep people in line, the Soviet Union had traditionally relied on force. This was seen in Hungary in 1956 and Czechoslovakia in 1968. Furthermore, the Brezhnev Doctrine stated that the Soviet Union would stop any attempts by Eastern Europe to relax communist control.

As part of his 'new thinking', Gorbachev wanted to change the way Eastern Europe was ruled:

- He saw it as morally wrong to use force to keep a population under control.

- He believed that giving greater freedom to Eastern Europe would strengthen communism rather than weaken it.

- The Soviet Union could no longer afford to keep large armies in Eastern Europe.

In 1988 Gorbachev rejected the Brezhnev Doctrine and said the countries of Eastern Europe would be free to do things in their own way without Soviet interference. This became known as the Sinatra Doctrine, in reference to the song 'My Way' popularised by the American singer Frank Sinatra. It had massive consequences: by 1990, all of the former communist regimes of Eastern Europe had been replaced by democratically elected governments.

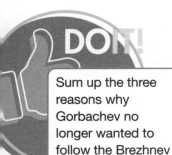

DO IT!

Sum up the three reasons why Gorbachev no longer wanted to follow the Brezhnev Doctrine.

The collapse of communism in Eastern Europe

Czechoslovakia

- In November 1989 mass demonstrations took place against communist rule.

- Known as the 'Velvet Revolution' because of their peaceful nature.

- These, together with the collapse of other communist regimes, forced the Communist Party to end one-party rule.

- In December 1989 a largely non-communist government was set up.

- The following year the Communist Party lost in democratic elections, gaining just 13 per cent of the vote.

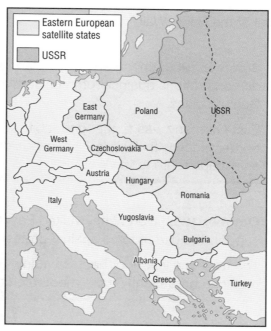

The end of communist rule in Eastern Europe

Poland

- The first East European country to end communist rule.

- In 1988 the independent trade union Solidarity organised huge strikes and demonstrations.

- Under growing pressure, the communist government agreed to democratic elections.

- Held in June 1989, these elections were a landslide victory for Solidarity.

East Germany

- Mass demonstrations helped force the government into reform.

- On 9 November 1989 people began destroying the Berlin Wall.

- The following month free elections were announced.

- The communists were heavily defeated in the 1990 elections.

Hungary

- The pressure for reform came from within the Communist Party.

- In 1988 János Kádár, the hard-line leader since 1956, was sacked.

- Inspired by Poland, talks took place between the Communist Party and opposition groups over the summer and autumn of 1989.

- In October 1989 the communist regime was formally abolished.

- The Communist Party lost the 1990 election.

Romania

- The only country to see serious violence in its revolution.

- The communist dictator, Ceausescu, refused to give up power.

- In December 1989 he was arrested and shot (with his wife) by anti-communist forces.

STRETCHIT!

1 To symbolise Hungary's move away from hard-line communism, Imry Nagy, leader of the 1956 revolution, was given a formal public funeral in June 1989.

2 Ceausescu was regarded as one of Europe's most hard-line communist dictators. Research Ceausescu's rule to find out more about him.

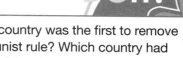

1 Which country was the first to remove communist rule? Which country had a peaceful revolution? Which country had a violent revolution?

2 Why could it be argued that 'people power' brought about the collapse of communism?

The fall of the Berlin Wall

Gorbachev's 'new thinking' set off a chain reaction of events that included the fall of the Berlin Wall.

Summer 1989: Encouraged by Poland's move to democracy, public demonstrations against communist rule started taking place in many East German cities.

East Germany was further de-stabilised when Hungary dismantled its border fence with Austria. Thousands of East Germans began using this as an escape route to the West.

October 1989: Gorbachev visited East Germany and said he would not support the use of force against protestors.

The hard-line leader of East Germany, Erich Honecker, resigned and was replaced by a slightly more moderate communist, Egon Krenz.

November 1989: Public demonstrations continued across East Germany, and the number of East Germans fleeing the country increased.

On 4 November over half a million people demonstrated in East Berlin.

On 9 November the East German government announced that East Germans would be able to travel freely to West Germany.

The Berlin Wall was now irrelevant and crowds starting demolishing it.

STRETCHIT!

In February 1989 Chris Gueffroy became the last person to be shot and killed while trying to escape across the Berlin Wall. Research the events surrounding his death, as well as the fate of the four German border guards involved in his killing.

The people of East and West Germany could now travel freely between the two countries and visit friends and relatives. Within the first two days of the wall falling, over two million people travelled from East to West Germany.

For 30 years the Berlin Wall had been a symbol of the Cold War, Soviet oppression and the division of Europe between communism and capitalism. Its destruction became a symbol that the Cold War was ending.

The significance of the fall of the Berlin Wall

The political shock of the Wall's fall led to the collapse of the East German government and paved the way for German reunification.

- In December 1989 Krenz, after barely two months in office, was replaced as East German leader by Hans Modrow, who promised free multi-party elections.

- On 15 January 1990, the hated Stasi's headquarters was stormed by protesters.

- Free elections were held on 18 March 1990 – the Communist Party was heavily defeated, gaining only 16 per cent of the vote.

- In October 1990 East and West Germany were formally reunited, with Berlin as the capital.

The end of the Warsaw Pact

The Warsaw Pact was formed in 1955 in order to protect the communist East from the capitalist West. When communist rule collapsed in Eastern Europe by 1989, the Warsaw Pact became both unnecessary and unwanted. Military cooperation ended in early 1990 and the Pact was formally dissolved in July 1991. This was significant for four reasons:

1 It was a clear sign that the Soviet Union was close to falling apart.

2 The Soviet Union had lost its main method of dominating Eastern Europe. When it had wanted to bring Czechoslovakia back into line in 1968 for example, it sent in Warsaw Pact forces.

3 Europe was no longer divided into two hostile armed groups – NATO and the Warsaw Pact.

4 All former Warsaw Pact countries have since joined NATO, a move not welcomed by Russia, the most powerful country to emerge from the collapse of the Soviet Union.

The collapse of the Soviet Union

The end of communist rule in Eastern Europe was quickly followed by the collapse of the Soviet Union.

The 15 republics of the Soviet Union

NAILIT!

Make sure you know the difference between the satellite states and the republics that made up the Soviet Union itself. Many students get confused by this!

Reasons for the collapse of the Soviet Union

1 **Eastern Europe:** The collapse of communism across Eastern Europe had a destabilising effect on the Soviet Union. Many of the Soviet Republics started pushing for their own independence. The Baltic states were the first to demand this in 1990, although Gorbachev did not initially agree.

2 Economy: The Soviet Union had major long-term economic problems. However Gorbachev's policy of Perestroika only made matters worse. Industrial output fell, prices rose and essential goods became scarce. By 1991 people were very angry about this, while the Soviet government itself had almost run out of money.

3 Glasnost: People used the policy of openness to criticise the Communist Party and Gorbachev. More and more people had the confidence to say that the Soviet Union had had its day.

4 *Coup d'etat:* In August 1991 there was an attempted *coup* by hard-line communists. Gorbachev was placed under house arrest, while troops moved into Moscow. The hardliners were defeated after three days because they were successfully opposed by Boris Yeltsin, leader of the Russian Soviet Republic. He urged soldiers to mutiny and workers to strike in protest.

The defeat of the *coup* contributed to the collapse of the Soviet Union in the following ways:

- It destroyed the authority of the Communist Party once and for all.

- Although Gorbachev resumed his position as leader, he no longer commanded much respect.

- Boris Yeltsin's popularity was boosted, but he hated communism and wanted to destroy the Soviet Union.

Gorbachev tried to stop the Soviet Union's collapse by promising greater freedom to the Republics in a new Union of Sovereign States. However the idea received little support. As a result, on Christmas Day 1991, Gorbachev made a special television broadcast announcing the end of the Soviet Union. As there was no longer a Soviet state to be president of, he also announced his own resignation. The Cold War was over.

The consequences of the Soviet Union's collapse

- Ten former Soviet Republics, including Russia, Belarus and the Ukraine, formed the Commonwealth of Independent States (CIS). This group of states loosely agreed to work together on mutual issues, including economics, defence and foreign policy.

- Some Soviet states decided to become fully independent and not join the CIS, including the Baltic States of Lithuania, Latvia and Estonia.

- The Cold War was now at an end. With the demise of the Soviet Union, there was no longer any ideological rivalry between East and West.

- Only one superpower remained: the USA.

DO IT!

1 Create a revision diagram, showing four major reasons for the collapse of the Soviet Union.

2 In just four sentences, sum up why the collapse of the Soviet Union was a significant event.

✓ CHECK IT!

1 Describe the 'three baskets' of the Helsinki Agreement.

2 Outline two results of the 'Reagan doctrine'.

3 Give two reasons to explain why Gorbachev was not willing to use force to maintain communist control over Eastern Europe.

4 Compare the different ways communism came to an end in Czechoslovakia and Romania.

How to answer the exam questions

There are three types of question for Section A on this paper:

1 Explain two consequences of a given event or development.

2 Write a narrative account analysing the key developments in a given period.

3 Explain the importance of two events or developments in the Cold War.

Edexcel exam-style questions

1 Explain **two** consequences of the Marshall Plan (1947). •
(Total for Question 1 = 8 marks)

> This is a consequence question. You need to explain two outcomes of the given event.

2 Write a narrative account analysing the key events of détente • during the 1970s.

> You may use the following in your answer:
>
> • The Helsinki Agreement (1975)
>
> • SALT 2 (1979)
>
> You **must** also use information of your own.

(Total for Question 2 = 8 marks)

> This is a narrative question. You have to link three events or developments together to form an overall story about a given period in the Cold War.

3 Explain **two** of the following: •

• The importance of the Soviet occupation of Eastern Europe (1945–48) for the early development of the Cold War.

• The importance of the Cuban Revolution (1959) for superpower relations.

• The importance of the Moscow Olympics boycott (1980) for relations between the Soviet Union and the USA.

(Total for Question 3 = 16 marks)

> This is an importance question. You are being asked to explain why two events mattered in the Cold War.

TOTAL FOR SECTION A = 32 marks

Section A: Question 1

Edexcel exam-style question

1 Explain **two** consequences of the Long Telegram (1946) for the development of the Cold War.

(Total for Question 1 = 8 marks)

The first question requires you to write about two consequences of an event in the Cold War.

The consequences of something are the results or effects of it.

So in this question you are **not** being asked to explain **why** an event happened, or even to **describe** that event. Your answer must **only** be focused on what happened as a **result** of that event. Ask yourself: What did it lead to? What were its consequences?

In the exam you should spend 12 minutes on this question, or six minutes per consequence. This is enough time to write one well explained paragraph for each consequence. Each consequence will be marked out of four, so give both answers equal attention.

You will be given half a page in the exam booklet for each consequence.

- Do not aim to include additional information on extra lines, even if you know a lot about the topic. As the maximum you can get for each consequence is four marks, this is not a high value question.

- Do not be tempted to merely rephrase the same consequence as your second answer, as this will not be credited.

Your answer will be marked in the following way, see mark scheme below.

- Assessment objective 1 (AO1) relates to historical knowledge and understanding.

- Assessment objective 2 (AO2) relates to the question focus; consequence.

- Each consequence will be marked out of four (2 × 4 marks).

Level	Mark	Simplified descriptor
	0	• Nothing deserving of a mark.
1	1–2	• The answer makes very simple or generalised comments about a consequence. (AO2) • Very little historical information is included. (AO1)
2	3–4	• A consequence is identified and explained. (AO2) • Specific historical information about the topic is included. (AO1)

NAILIT!

Don't spend more than 12 minutes answering question 1 – any more time will mean that you don't leave enough time for the rest of the questions.

You could use the self-check table below as a quick way to make sure that your answer achieves high marks.

I have...	✓ or ✗
Identified two different consequences.	
Explained each consequence.	
Included some precise, relevant knowledge such as names, dates, events.	

DO IT!

Identifying consequences

Here are some events and their consequences but they are mixed up.

Match the key Cold War event to one of its consequences.

	Event			Consequence
1	Tehran Conference (1943)		A	NATO was formed in order to prevent Soviet expansion.
2	Novikov Telegram (1946)		B	Castro declared that he was a communist.
3	Marshall Plan (1947)		C	Britain and the USA agreed to open a second front in France in 1944.
4	Berlin Crisis (1948)		D	East and West Germany were reunited in 1990.
5	Hungarian Uprising (1956)		E	The Brezhnev Doctrine was replaced by the Sinatra Doctrine.
6	Berlin Ultimatum (1958)		F	Tensions between the USA and the Soviet Union were significantly reduced.
7	The Bay of Pigs incident (1961)		G	Western Europe benefited from $13 billion of aid.
8	The Prague Spring (1968)		H	This confirmed Stalin's fears about an aggressive USA.
9	Helsinki Agreement (1975)		I	Around 200,000 Hungarians fled the country.
10	Gorbachev's appointment as Soviet leader (1985)		J	A whole class of intermediate range nuclear weapons were scrapped.
11	The INF Treaty (1987)		K	Warsaw Pact armies invaded Czechoslovakia in August 1968.
12	Fall of the Berlin Wall (1989)		L	Summits were held to discuss the 'Berlin problem'.

 # DOIT!

Here are some causes, main events and consequences of the US boycott of the 1980 Moscow Olympics.

Decide which of the statements are causes (CA), main events (E) and consequences (CO).

	CA/E/CO
A The Soviet Union came top of the medal table with 80 golds	
B The Soviet Union were angry because the Moscow Games were made to look second rate when 65 countries did not attend.	
C In December 1979 the Soviet Union invaded Afghanistan, which angered the USA.	
D The boycott showed that all the goodwill built up during the period of détente in the 1970s was gone.	
E An alternative sporting event was held in the USA called the Liberty Bell Classic.	
F Carter, the US President, wanted to punish the Soviet Union because of the invasion.	
G Carter took many measures against the Soviet Union, including scrapping SALT 2, economic sanctions and pulling the USA out of the Olympics.	
H In response to the US boycott, the Soviet Union refused to attend the 1984 Los Angeles Olympics.	
I East Germany came second in the medal table with 47 golds.	
J It showed that the Cold War was so bad it was damaging sporting events.	

Question 1: Sample questions and answers

 ### Edexcel exam-style question

1 Explain **two** consequences of the construction of the Berlin Wall (1961).

(Total for Question 1 = 8 marks)

After reading the question, take a moment to identify some consequences of the event. You could make a list or draw a spider diagram, as the student has done below. You will then need to pick two of these consequences to write about in your answer.

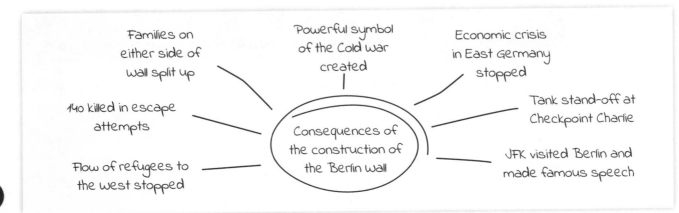

Sample answer 1

Consequence 1:

The Berlin Wall was mainly made of concrete and stretched for 96 miles around West Berlin. The East Germans made it almost impossible to get over the wall by adding barbed wire, a death strip, watchtowers, searchlights and regular foot patrols with attack dogs.

This answer contains accurate historical knowledge but it is too descriptive. It does not put forward a clear consequence. This answer would be better if the student used some of this information to explain how, for example, the Wall permanently divided the city of Berlin and its people.

Consequence 2:

There was a stand-off between US and Soviet tanks at the main crossing point of the Berlin Wall, called Checkpoint Charlie. The Soviet tanks were T-55s and the American tanks were M-48s.

The tank stand-off is a good choice for a consequence, but it is too brief. It could be developed further by explaining the short-term spike it caused in Cold War tensions. The tank information is interesting but not relevant to answering this question.

1 Using the mark scheme on page 56, what mark would you give sample answer 1 above?

2 Have a go at answering this question yourself. When you have finished, double check your answer by using the self-check table on page 57, and then read sample answer 2 below, which is a very good answer.

Sample answer 2

Language is used to clearly show a consequence is being introduced.

Consequence 1:

One consequence was a short-term rise in Cold War tensions. The Americans were angry about the wall. They also said East German guards at the wall had no right to check American identity documents. As a result, the USA brought tanks up to Checkpoint Charlie in October 1961, and the Soviets then did the same. They faced each other for 16 hours and there was concern that war could break out. Eventually the tanks were withdrawn and this short crisis passed.

A consequence is clearly identified and introduced.

NAILIT!

You must write about two consequences of the event given in the question. You won't get any marks for writing about more than two consequences. The two consequences **must** be different.

Precise, relevant historical knowledge is then given to explain this point. The tank stand-off is a good example to use.

Consequence 2:

The building of the Berlin Wall led to a lot of suffering. Families were split up and travel restrictions made it difficult for relatives to see one another. Some people tried to escape across the wall but this was dangerous. Over 140 people were killed by East German border guards, including Peter Fechter in 1962. After being shot, he was denied medical treatment and he bled to death in the death strip.

Another important consequence is clearly introduced in the first sentence so the reader knows the focus of the answer.

The detail about Peter Fechter is a good example of precise, relevant historical knowledge.

Edexcel exam-style question

1 Explain **two** consequences of the the Truman Doctrine (1947).

(Total for Question 1 = 8 marks)

To help get you started on this question, use the spider diagram to remind yourself of some of the main consequences of the Truman Doctrine. You will then need to pick two of these consequences to write about in your answer.

NAILIT!

Use key phrases such as 'this led to', 'as a result', 'as a consequence', 'the effect of this was' in your answer to show that you are clearly linking the event with a consequence.

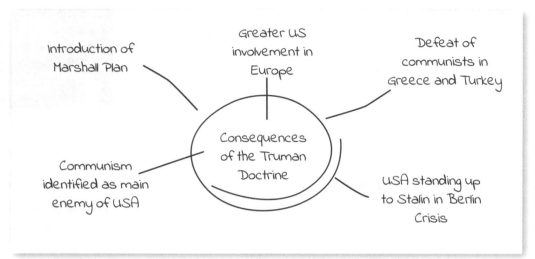

Introduction of Marshall Plan

Greater US involvement in Europe

Defeat of communists in Greece and Turkey

Consequences of the Truman Doctrine

Communism identified as main enemy of USA

USA standing up to Stalin in Berlin Crisis

Sample answer 3

This answer does not focus enough on a consequence. For example, the third and fourth sentences explain the causes of the Truman Doctrine, which is not relevant. Only the last sentence mentions a consequence, but this needs much more development. To improve, the student needs to explain why the Truman Doctrine made the Cold War worse.

Consequence 1:

The Truman Doctrine had important consequences for the Cold War. In 1947 Truman said the USA would use its economic and military resources to stop the expansion of communism. The Truman Doctrine came about because the Soviet Union had taken over much of Eastern Europe. Also Truman was worried that Stalin wanted to take over western Europe. As a result, the Truman Doctrine led to the Cold War getting worse.

DOIT!

Using the feedback provided, try to improve this answer. When you are happy with your attempt, double check it using the self-check table on page 57 and then read sample answer 4 on page 61, which gives a much better answer to this question.

Consequence 2:

In 1948 Stalin blockaded Berlin. Truman did not want west Berlin to fall to the communists and so ordered food and other supplies to be flown into the city. The airlift lasted 11 months. Eventually Stalin had to admit defeat and he ended the blockade. West Berlin therefore stayed under western control.

This answer contains historically accurate information. However, the focus of the question is on consequences of the Truman Doctrine and the student does not clearly explain how the Berlin airlift is linked to the Truman Doctrine. The answer therefore misses its target. It would be much better if the student explained that the Berlin Blockade was the first real test of the Truman Doctrine. Truman was therefore determined to prove his policy and so ordered the hugely ambitious airlift.

Sample answer 4

Consequence 1:

One consequence was the defeat of a communist uprising in Greece. The Greek government had been fighting the communists since 1944 with British help. However, in 1947 Britain warned that it would be unable to continue helping due to lack of money. The USA, however, stepped in because the Truman Doctrine said that it would support any country threatened with communist takeover. This US support, mainly in the form of money, led to the defeat of the communist rebels and Greece became a strong US ally as a result.

Good first sentence. It contains the key word 'consequence' from the question and it also gives the theme of the paragraph, 'defeat of the uprisings'.

The final two sentences clearly link the communist uprising to the focus of the question, the consequence of the Truman Doctrine.

The answer is developed over the second and third sentences with relevant historical information.

Consequence 2:

One result was the Marshall Plan. The aim of the Truman Doctrine was to stop communist expansion. However, US Secretary of State George Marshall realised that communism was growing in popularity in western Europe because of poverty after the war. In response he developed a huge aid programme called the Marshall Plan. From 1948 $13 billion in aid was given to western Europe. This led to economic recovery and higher living standards, and as a result communism became less popular.

'One result' is a good opening phrase, as it directly focuses on consequence.

These sentences clearly explain the link between the Truman Doctrine, poverty in Europe and the Marshall Plan.

Contains detailed, relevant historical knowledge.

Section A: Question 2

Question 2 focuses on an important period in the Cold War. This could cover several years or a much shorter period.

Edexcel exam-style question

2 Write a narrative account analysing the key events of the Prague Spring (1968).

> You may use the following in your answer:
> - The policy of 'socialism with a human face'
> - The Soviet invasion
>
> You **must** also use information of your own.

(Total for Question 2 = 8 marks)

You will need to write an 'analytical narrative'. This is an answer that not only describes what happened, but also finds connections and makes sense of events as they unfolded.

It is perhaps easier to think of an analytical narrative as writing a story. Like any good story, your answer needs a beginning, then development and finally an end:

- The first thing to do is make sure you are clear on the overall focus of the question. What is the narrative designed to analyse?

  - Next, select three points that can form an overall sequence of events. These will be the three paragraphs of your answer.
  - If a date range is specified in the question, make sure your three points are all within this.
  - It is important to make sure your three points are spread across the given date range. In other words, don't have three points all from the beginning or from the end of the time period.
  - To help you, two stimulus points will be provided in the question. You do not need to use these, but they are still useful reminders of either important events along the narrative or the chronological span of the question.

- Ensure you write about the events in the correct chronological order.

- When you write about each event, bring in relevant detailed historical knowledge.

- As you are creating an analytical narrative, it is important that you explain how each event links to the next one. The best way of doing this is using linking words such as 'as a result', 'because of', and 'as a consequence'.

NAILIT!

Great linking words to include in your answer are: 'as a result'; 'this led to'; 'despite this'; 'in contrast'; 'therefore'; 'because'; 'in order to'; 'as a consequence'; 'combined with'.

In the exam you should spend 12 minutes on this question. This is enough time to write three paragraphs, covering three linked points. You will be given two pages in the exam booklet.

Your answer will be marked in the following way.

- Assessment objective 1 (AO1) relates to historical knowledge and understanding.

- Assessment objective 2 (AO2) relates to the question focus; an analytical narrative covering causation/consequence/change.

Level	Mark	Simplified descriptor
	0	• Nothing deserving of a mark.
1	1–2	• A basic outline of events is provided, but the events are probably not in the correct order and no links are made. (AO2) • Very little historical information is included. (AO1)
2	3–4	• A narrative is given, made up of a sequence of events in chronological order leading to an outcome. (AO2) • Some attempt is made to make links between the sequence of events. (AO2) • Some passages may not be clearly explained. (AO2) • Some accurate and relevant historical information is included, but more is needed. (AO1) *NOTE: Answers that do not provide three distinct points cannot get more than 4 marks.*
3	6–8	• A narrative is given, consisting of a clear sequence of events in chronological order, leading to an outcome. (AO2) • The answer clearly explains the links between the sequence of events. (AO2) • The answer is easy to understand and makes sense. (AO2) • Accurate and relevant historical information is included. (AO1)

Use the self-check table below as a quick way to check your answer reaches the higher marks.

I have...	✓ or ✗
Included three points over three paragraphs.	
Put the points in the correct chronological order.	
Used linking words and identified connections when moving from one point to the next.	
Explained each point over several sentences.	
Included some precise, relevant knowledge for each point.	

NAILIT!

Don't spend more than 12 minutes answering question 2 – any more time will mean that you don't leave enough time for the final question.

Identifying and ordering events

Once three events or points have been identified, you need to be able to put them into the correct chronological order.

DO IT!

The table (right) gives three important periods of the Cold War. There are five events related to each of these periods (listed A to O in the table below) but they are all jumbled up.

Complete the table in chronological order using the events listed A to O.

Early tensions between East and West, 1943–47					
Tensions over Berlin 1958–63					
The collapse of Soviet control over Eastern Europe, 1985–91					

A Gorbachev issues the Sinatra Doctrine	**F** Tehran Conference	**K** First test of the US atomic bomb
B The Novikov Telegram	**G** Kennedy visits Berlin	**L** Solidarity wins the 1989 Polish elections
C Paris Summit collapses	**H** Vienna Summit between Khrushchev and Kennedy	**M** Berlin Wall built
D East and West Germany reunited	**I** Fall of the Berlin Wall	**N** Poland becomes a Soviet satellite state
E The Warsaw Pact formally ended	**J** Yalta Conference	**O** Khrushchev issues the Berlin Ultimatum

Mini narrative chains

In your answers to question 2, you need to build a narrative chain by explaining how the three events link together. Read the two chains below.

Chain 1: The main developments in Eastern Europe, 1944–47

At Yalta Stalin promised to hold free elections in Eastern Europe, which greatly pleased the West.

Despite this promise, elections were rigged and countries like Poland became Soviet satellite states.

As a result of the Soviet occupation of Eastern Europe, Truman issued the Truman Doctrine, promising to stop further communist expansion.

Chain 2: The key events of détente in the 1970s

SALT 1 was the first great success of détente, slowing down the arms race by limiting the number of nuclear missile launchers.

After SALT 1, further agreements included the Helsinki Agreements, which encouraged trade and cultural links between East and West.

Despite these successes, the Soviet invasion of Afghanistan brought efforts to improve relations to an end and a new Cold War set in.

DO IT!

1 Complete the missing sections in chains 3 and 4 below. (HINTS: the Berlin airlift would make an ideal third point for Chain 3; the end of the Warsaw Pact could be a good choice for Chain 4.)

2 Write your own mini narrative chains for the following topics:

- The development of the Cold War, 1947–49
- The key events of the Prague Spring, 1968.

NAIL IT!

Make sure each point links to the next one to show how the events are linked together.

Remember to select **three** events – you can use the two given in the bullet points of the question but you don't have to.

Chain 3: The key events of the Berlin Crisis, 1948–49

| Stalin was worried that the Western powers were trying to build up the western part of Germany into a powerful country that would eventually invade the Soviet Union. | As a result, in 1948 Stalin decided to try and remove the Western powers from Berlin by blockading the western part of the city. | _____ _____ |

Chain 4: The key developments in Eastern Europe between 1988 and 1991

| In 1988 Gorbachev replaced the Brezhnev Doctrine with the Sinatra Doctrine, which stated that the Soviet Union would no longer interfere in Eastern Europe. | As a result of this huge policy change, in 1989 communist governments across Eastern Europe came to an end, starting initially in Poland with the election of Solidarity. | _____ _____ |

Question 2: Sample questions and answers

Edexcel exam-style question

2 Write a narrative account analysing the main developments in the Grand Alliance in the years 1943–45.

You may use the following in your answer:

- The Tehran Conference (1943)

- The Potsdam Conference (1945)

You **must** also use information of your own.

(Total for Question 2 = 8 marks)

Sample answer 1

The Big Three met at Potsdam in 1945. There was a lot of tension between Stalin and the new US President, Truman. This is because Truman hated Stalin. In the meeting Truman also tried to intimidate Stalin by telling him about the atomic bomb. This angered the Soviet leader and made him worried that the USA had long-term plans to invade the Soviet Union. Potsdam was not a success and there were no further meetings of the Grand Alliance after this.

This answer contains accurate knowledge about the Yalta and Potsdam conferences. However it would not score highly because:

- There are no links between each point.
- A third point has not been added.
- The points are not in chronological order.

In 1945 the Big Three met at Yalta. This was a key moment for the Grand Alliance because they had almost defeated Nazi Germany. They therefore turned their attention to what should happen after the war. A lot was agreed. For example, they agreed to set up the United Nations. They agreed to divide Germany into occupation zones and prosecute Nazi war criminals. It is easy to see why this Conference was seen as a success.

DO IT!

Have a go at improving sample answer 1 above. When you have finished give your answer the final seal of approval by using the self-check table on page 63. You can also compare it to sample answer 2 below which is a very good answer.

Sample answer 2

The first formal meeting of the Grand Alliance was in Tehran in 1943. The Big Three of Stalin, Roosevelt and Churchill mainly discussed how to win the war against Nazi Germany. There were some tensions over military strategy. Stalin wanted Britain and the USA to quickly open a second front in France. He was angry that this would not happen until May 1944. However, the need to stay united in the fight against Hitler meant that this disagreement did not become a major issue.

As Germany was close to defeat in 1945, a further conference was held at Yalta. Its main purpose was to discuss post-war plans. There were lots of agreements. It was decided to split Germany up into four zones of occupation. It was agreed that Nazi war criminals would be prosecuted. Stalin promised to hold free elections in Eastern Europe. This conference was widely seen as a success for the Grand Alliance.

The answer is well organised in three separate paragraphs. Each paragraph gives one point/event, and the points are in the correct chronological order. The second paragraph gives a third point from the student's own knowledge. The points are linked together, showing a clear sequence of events. Detailed, relevant historical knowledge is included to support each point.

The good relations seen at Yalta, however, were not to last. When the Big Three met at Potsdam in August 1945, relations were very strained. Roosevelt had died and the new US President, Truman, hated Stalin and communism. Britain and the USA opposed Stalin's plan to take massive reparations from Germany. They were also unhappy about the lack of free elections in Eastern Europe. The Potsdam Conference can be seen as the point when the Grand Alliance ended.

Edexcel exam-style question

2 Write a narrative account analysing the key events of the Hungarian Uprising (1956).

You may use the following in your answer:

- Matyas Rakosi

- The Soviet invasion

You **must** also use information of your own.

(Total for Question 2 = 8 marks)

Before starting to write your answer it is worth spending a few minutes on a brief plan. This will help ensure your answer is well organised and you don't leave anything out. Here is one student's sample plan:

Paragraph 1: Reasons why Hungarians hated communist rule - Rakosi's unpopularity, secret police and poor living standards.

Paragraph 2: Link from Rakosi's unpopularity to being replaced by Nagy. Nagy's reforms - end one-party rule, freedom of speech, free elections, leave Warsaw Pact.

Paragraph 3: Link from Nagy's reforms to Soviet invasion. Impact of the invasion - bitter fighting, 2500 killed, 200,000 fled, Nagy executed, Uprising crushed.

DO IT!

Before looking at sample answer 3 below, have a go at answering the exam-style question above for yourself. You can use the plan (left) to help you. When you have finished, don't forget to use the self-check table on page 63 to quality control your answer.

Sample answer 3

The Hungarian Uprising was caused by the unpopularity of the communist government. Its leader, Rakosi, was particularly hated. He was a hard-line communist like Stalin. He established a feared secret police called the AVH and he arrested all his political opponents. Rakosi was also unpopular because living standards in Hungary had fallen and he allowed a lot of Hungary's food to be sent to the Soviet Union.

Rakosi's unpopularity led to large scale protests in Hungary in 1956. In order to calm the situation the Soviet Union installed a new communist leader called Nagy. However, Nagy was encouraged by the protest movement and started making radical reforms. He said he would end one-party communist rule and introduce free elections and freedom of speech. He also said Hungary would leave the Warsaw Pact.

Nagy's radical plans resulted in a Soviet invasion. Khrushchev was not prepared to let any country leave the Warsaw Pact, as the security of the Soviet Union depended on it. On 4 November 1956 Soviet soldiers and tanks invaded Hungary and after bitter fighting crushed the uprising. Around 2500 Hungarians were killed and 200,000 fled the country. Nagy was arrested and executed. The Hungarian Uprising therefore ended in failure.

This answer clearly tells the story of the Hungarian Uprising, covering its causes, main events and ultimate failure due to Soviet invasion. In addition:

- The points are in the correct chronological order.
- Detailed, relevant historical knowledge is included.
- The points are linked together, showing a clear sequence of events.
- A third point has been added.

Section A: Question 3

The third question comprises two 8-mark questions based on the idea of importance.

Edexcel exam-style question

3 Explain **two** of the following:

- The importance of the Marshall Plan (1947) for the development of the Cold War. **(8)**
- The importance of SALT 1 (1972) for superpower relations. **(8)**
- The importance of the end of the Warsaw Pact (1991) for relations between the USA and the Soviet Union. **(8)**

(Total for Question 3 = 16 marks)

Question 3 assesses your ability to explain why an event, person or development was important for a further factor. This means that you are **not** being asked to explain **why** an event happened, or even to **describe** that event. There is no point including information relating to these areas.

- In the exam you will be given a choice of three questions. You must pick **two** of them. It is best to pick the two that you know most about.

- As a general guide, aim to explain two to three distinct ways the event/person/development was important for the further factor.

- A phrase like 'This was important because...' is helpful to keep your writing focused on the question.

- Remember to use detailed historical knowledge when explaining your answer.

In total you should spend 25 minutes on this question. Divide this equally between both answers. You will be given two pages in the exam for each answer.

This question is worth 16 marks. Each part of the answer will be marked out of 8 and will be marked in the following way:

- Assessment objective 1 (AO1) relates to historical knowledge and understanding.

- Assessment objective 2 (AO2) relates to the question focus; consequence and significance.

Level	Mark	Simplified descriptor
	0	• Nothing deserving of a mark.
1	1–2	• The answer does not focus on importance. (AO2) • Lengthy descriptions may be provided. (AO2) • Limited information about the topic is included. (AO1)
2	3–4	• The answer shows some focus on importance but the comments on importance are not always linked to the further factor. (AO2) • Some reasoning is included in the answer. (AO2) • Some parts of the answer may be poorly explained. (AO2) • Some accurate and relevant historical information is included, but more is needed. (AO1)
3	6–8	• The answer is fully focused on importance in relation to the further factor. (AO2) • The answer is well reasoned. (AO2) • The answer is easy to understand and makes sense. (AO2) • Accurate and relevant historical information is included. (AO1)

You could use the self-check table below as a quick way to make sure that your answer achieves high marks.

I have...	✓ or ✗
Used the key words from the question in my answer.	
Identified 2–3 ways the event/development was important for the further factor.	
Explained each of my points over several sentences.	
Included some precise, relevant knowledge for each point.	

Thinking about importance

In question 3 of the Superpower relations exam, you will need to explain why a key moment in the Cold War was important. For example, in answer to the question, 'Why was the Yalta Conference important for the Grand Alliance?' You might consider that they agreed on dividing up Germany and creating a United Nations but disagreed about Poland's new government and about reparations.

The table below gives one reason why some Cold War events were important for US-Soviet relations.

Cold War event	Why it was important for relations between the superpowers.
Creation of Soviet satellite states, 1945–48	The West saw this as evidence that Stalin wanted to take over the world.
Marshall Plan, 1947	Stalin attacked it as 'dollar imperialism.'
Formation of NATO, 1949	Stalin saw it as an aggressive military alliance directed against the Soviet Union.
Building of the Berlin Wall, 1961	The Wall became a symbol of cold war divisions
Cuban Missile Crisis, 1962	The USA and Soviet Union came close to nuclear war – this led to a new hotline to prevent this from happening again.
Prague Spring, 1968	The West was angry that a movement for democratic reform had been crushed by the Warsaw Pact.
Gorbachev's 'new thinking'	Gorbachev wanted to end the arms race, which led to the INF Treaty.
Strategic Defence Initiative, 1983	It showed that the USA was determined to win the arms race against the Soviet Union.
Fall of the Berlin Wall, 1989	It showed the Soviet Union would no longer use force to keep control over its satellite states, which dramatically improved relations with the West.

DO IT!

Give two more reasons why each Cold War event in the table on the right was important for relations between the superpowers.

NAIL IT!

To determine the importance of something, ask yourself: Why does this event matter? What difference did it make to the further factor?

Here is an exam question and a sample answer on the importance of the invasion of Afghanistan for the Cold War. The sentences in the answer are in the wrong order.

Edexcel exam-style question

- Explain the importance of the Soviet invasion of Afghanistan (1979) for the ongoing Cold War between the USA and the Soviet Union. (8)

A Firstly, it ended the period of détente.	
B Thirdly, it led to indirect fighting between the Soviet Union and the USA.	
C Cooperation came to an end after the invasion and an important arms control treaty called SALT 2 was scrapped.	
D The Soviet invasion was therefore important in making the Cold War much more serious.	
E The invasion of Afghanistan was really significant for the ongoing Cold War because it made it much worse.	
F Carter said the USA would use force to protect its interests in the Persian Gulf region.	
G This is because the USA started supplying weapons to the mujahideen, who were fighting the Soviets.	
H This showed the USA now had a much more hostile attitude to the Soviet Union and was even prepared to go to war.	
I This had seen a thaw in the Cold War in the 1970s, with both sides agreeing to respect human rights in the 1975 Helsinki Agreement, for example.	
J Secondly, it led to the Carter Doctrine.	

1 Highlight the three reasons for importance given in the answer above.

2 Order the sentences A–J in the right hand column so they are in the correct order to give a great answer.

3 The Soviet invasion of Afghanistan had a huge impact on the Cold War. Note down two additional consequences not covered by this answer.

Below is another student's answer to the same question.

The incident mattered a lot for superpower relations mainly because it made relations better. This is because, firstly, it led Batista to become a capitalist. Cuba and the Soviet Union then became close allies. This angered the USA because they did not want a communist state in their 'backyard'. Secondly, Brezhnev started a military build-up in Cuba following the incident. He said he wanted to protect the island from Soviet aggression. He sent Cuba lots of weapons including aircraft carriers. Their discovery by American UB40 spy planes sparked the Cuban Naval Crisis. Finally, Truman was made to look foolish for allowing the Bay of Pigs invasion to happen. As a result, he became more determined to stand up to the USSR to prove himself. For example, when Soviet missile sites were found on Cuba in 1965, he was determined to win the crisis, even though it pushed the world to the brink of nuclear war.

This student has written what could be a superb answer to an importance question on Cuba. Find and correct the ten factual mistakes.

Question 3: Sample questions and answers

Edexcel exam-style question

- Explain the importance of the Berlin Crisis (1948) for the development of the Cold War.

(8)

Sample answer 1

DO IT!

Try rewriting sample answer 1, making as many improvements as you can. When you have finished, check your answer using the self-check table on page 69. You can also compare your answer to the better answer given in sample answer 2 below.

Although accurate, the student has not linked this knowledge to the focus of the question which is 'the development of the Cold War'

The Berlin Crisis started on the 24 June 1948 when Stalin closed all road and rail access to West Berlin. Two million people lived in this part of the city and they were now entirely cut off. It can be seen as important because this was the first big crisis of the Cold War and it showed that the Grand Alliance was over. Stalin now saw the West as his enemy. It was also important because in some ways the Berlin Crisis reduced Cold War tensions. This is because it ended the emigration of huge numbers of skilled workers from East Germany. This had been a major source of tension between the two sides in the lead up to the Berlin Crisis.

This sentence directly addresses the question and makes a valid point.

The student has mixed up the Berlin Crisis with the events surrounding the construction of the Berlin Wall. This is easily done, so make sure you are writing about the correct Berlin incident!

Sample answer 2

The Berlin Crisis was very important for the development of the Cold War. Firstly, Stalin's decision to blockade the city made the West angry. It confirmed their view that Stalin was aggressive and wanted to spread communism. Secondly, it ended hopes of the superpowers cooperating over the future of Germany. Instead, Germany was permanently divided into two: the capitalist Federal Republic and the communist Democratic Republic. This was never the intention of the Big Three at the end of the Second World War; they had wanted to keep Germany united. Finally, the Berlin Crisis led to the formation of NATO in 1949. The West claimed NATO was a defensive alliance, but the Soviet Union saw it as an aggressive alliance and as a result they expanded their own military and later formed the Warsaw Pact. The Berlin Crisis therefore made the Cold War much worse.

This is an analytical answer because it is focused throughout on answering the question. There is no irrelevant material on the causes of the Berlin Crisis or the airlift itself. Instead, the answer explains three clear ways the Berlin Crisis mattered for the Cold War. Each reason is supported by some specific knowledge.

Edexcel exam-style question

- Explain the importance of the Soviet invasion of Afghanistan for relations between the superpowers.

(8)

You may find it helpful to write a list or spider diagram of points before you write your answer, as this student has done below.

SALT 2 not passed

End of détente

Olympic boycotts

Impact of Soviet invasion of Afghanistan on superpower relations

Carter Doctrine

US sanctions on Soviet Union

Increase in US military spending

DO IT!

Have a go at answering this question on the importance of the Soviet invasion of Afghanistan. When you have finished your answer, make use of the self-check table on page 69 and then compare your answer to sample answer 3 below, which is a very good answer.

Sample answer 3

The Soviet invasion of Afghanistan was massively important in changing the relationship between the superpowers. First, this is because it brought to an end the period of good superpower relations known as détente. This had led to some significant agreements such as SALT 1 and the Helsinki Agreement. However, after the invasion the USA no longer trusted the USSR. Second, it meant that a landmark arms control treaty called SALT 2 was not passed by the US government. This treaty would have led to actual cuts in the number of nuclear missile launchers, but after the invasion the American government did not want to sign it. Third, the invasion mattered because it led to a brand new US foreign policy called the Carter Doctrine. This said the USA would use force to stop Soviet expansion into the Persian Gulf region. As a result, the invasion of Afghanistan had a big negative impact on superpower relations.

This answer uses key words from the question and uses language to clearly signpost the start of each new point. It gives three distinct points on how this event changed superpower relations. It includes relevant, precise details to show the student's knowledge.

NAIL IT!

Always support your answer with detailed, relevant historical knowledge.

Edexcel exam-style question

- Explain the importance of the USA's development of the atomic bomb for relations between the superpowers in the years 1945–49. (8)

Sample answer 4

The USA's development of the atomic bomb was important in worsening superpower relations. First, it made the Americans behave more aggressively to the Soviet Union. This was seen at the Potsdam Conference of 1945, when Truman was very tough in his negotiations with Stalin. As a result, few agreements were reached. Second, it made Stalin feel worried because he did not have an atomic bomb. As a result he became more determined to protect the Soviet Union in other ways. This led him to occupy Eastern Europe between 1945 and 1948 and turn it into a buffer zone. This action, however, angered the USA. Finally, it led to the arms race. The Soviets started working on their own atomic bomb, completing it in 1949. Following this, each side looked to build more powerful bombs. The atomic bomb therefore caused superpower relations to spiral downhill.

DO IT!

Have a go at answering the exam-style question above for yourself. When you have finished, quality control your work with the self-check table on page 69 and read sample answer 4 (right), which is a very good response.

This is an effective answer because:

- Clear language is used to signpost the start of each new point.
- It explains three ways the atomic bomb mattered for superpower relations.
- All the points are within the date range.
- The student clearly knows the topic well and brings in some good historical knowledge.

Practice papers

Practice paper 1: Section A

Answer ALL questions.

1 Explain **two** consequences of Gorbachev's 'new thinking' on Eastern Europe.

(Total for Question 1 = 8 marks)

2 Write a narrative account analysing the main developments in US-Soviet relations in the years 1947–49.

> You may use the following in your answer:
> - Truman Doctrine (1947)
> - Formation of NATO (1949)
>
> You **must** also use information of your own.

(Total for Question 2 = 8 marks)

3 Explain **two** of the following:
- The importance of the Potsdam Conference (1945) for the early development of the Cold War.

  (8)
- The importance of the events in Hungary in 1956 for international relations.

  (8)
- The importance of the Cuban Missile Crisis (1962) for superpower relations.

  (8)

(Total for Question 3 = 16 marks)

TOTAL FOR SECTION A = 32 marks

Practice paper 2: Section A

Answer ALL questions.

1 Explain **two** consequences of the 1959 Cuban Revolution.

(Total for Question 1 = 8 marks)

2 Write a narrative account analysing the key developments in the collapse of Soviet control over Eastern Europe in the years 1988–91.

> You may use the following in your answer:
> - The fall of the Berlin Wall, 1989
> - The end of the Warsaw Pact, 1991
>
> You **must** also use information of your own.

(Total for Question 2 = 8 marks)

3 Explain **two** of the following:
- The importance of NATO for the development of the Cold War. (8)
- The importance of the construction of the Berlin Wall (1961) for tensions between East and West. (8)
- The importance of SALT 1 for relations between the USA and the Soviet Union. (8)

(Total for Question 3 = 16 marks)

TOTAL FOR SECTION A = 32 marks

Doing well in your exam

This revision guide is designed to help you with your **Paper 2: Period Study Section A** exam.

Assessment objectives

Your answers will be marked according to a mark scheme based on four assessment objectives (AOs). AOs are set by Ofqual and are the same across all GCSE History specifications and all exam boards:

AO1	demonstrate knowledge and understanding of the key features and characteristics of the period studied.
AO2	explain and analyse historical events and periods studied using second-order historical concepts (cause and consequence).
AO3	analyse, evaluate and use sources (contemporary to the period) to make substantiated judgements, in the context of historical events studied.
AO4	analyse, evaluate and make substantiated judgements about interpretations (including how and why interpretations may differ) in the context of historical events studied.

Paper 2 Section A, covered in this guide, examines AO1 and AO2.

You must <u>revise all of the content</u> from the specification as the questions in your exam could be on *any* of the topics listed. This guide is modelled on the specification so make sure you cover **all** the topics in this book.

There are three different types of question to answer in Paper 2 Section A:

Question 1	The first question requires you to write about **two** consequences of an event in the Cold War. The consequences of something are the results or effects of it.
Best answers …	will only be focused on what happened as a result of that event.
(8 marks) *12 minutes*	The answer carries 8 marks. Each consequence will be marked out of 4, so give both answers equal attention. You should spend 12 minutes on this question, or six minutes per consequence.
Question 2	This question focuses on an important period in the Cold War. This could cover several years or a much shorter period. You will need to write an 'analytical narrative'. This is an answer that not only describes what happened, but also finds connections and makes sense of events as they unfolded.
Best answers …	will cover three events in three paragraphs, all in chronological order. As you are creating an analytical narrative, it is important that you explain how each event links to the next one.
(8 marks) *12 minutes*	This question is worth 8 marks. You should aim to spend 12 minutes on this question.

Question 3	The third question comprises two 8-mark questions based on the idea of importance. You will need to explain why an event, person or development was important for a further factor. In the exam you will be given a choice of **three** questions. You must pick **two** of them. It is best to pick the two that you know most about.
Best answers …	will explain two to three distinct ways the event/person/development was important for the further factor.
(16 marks) *25 minutes*	This question is worth 16 marks. In total you should spend 25 minutes on this question. Divide your time equally between both answers.

Find past papers and mark schemes, and specimen papers on the Edexcel website at www.qualifications.pearson.com for further practice.

Glossary

annexation The illegal takeover of another country.

anti-ballistic missile A weapon designed to intercept and destroy ballistic missiles.

CIA The US government's main spy service.

coalition government A government made up of two or more political parties working together.

congress The branch of the US government responsible for passing laws.

containment The US policy of 'containing' communism by stopping it spreading.

coup d'etat Armed revolt against the existing government.

deploy To move troops, weapons and equipment into position for military action.

de-Stalinisation Ending the harsh and repressive policies associated with Stalin.

diplomat An official whose job is to represent one country in another, and who usually works in an **embassy**.

economic sanctions A way of punishing a country by imposing limits on their international trade.

embassy The official residence of a foreign government in another country.

fall out The radioactive dust that falls to Earth when a nuclear weapon explodes.

freedom of assembly The right to organise meetings and protests.

General Secretary The official name for the leader of the Soviet Union.

ICBM Intercontinental ballistic missile. A nuclear missile capable of travelling 5500 km or more and hitting other continents.

imperialism A system in which a country rules over other countries.

Jupiter missile A medium range nuclear missile.

the Kremlin A group of buildings in Moscow that contained the most important parts of the Soviet government.

launchers Sometimes referred to as delivery vehicles, nuclear weapons could either be launched from silos in the ground, from the back of mobile vehicles, from submarine launch tubes or dropped from a heavy bomber.

left-wing A left-wing person or group supports the political aims of groups such as socialists and communists.

MIRV Multiple independently targetable re-entry vehicle. A missile containing several nuclear warheads, each capable of hitting a different target.

nationalise When the state takes control of privately owned businesses and property.

nuclear monopoly From 1945–49, the USA was the only country to possess nuclear weapons.

the Pentagon The Headquarters of the United States Department of Defence.

people's democracies The communist countries of Eastern Europe.

Red Army The army of the Soviet Union.

reparations Compensation, either in the form of money or industrial equipment, for wartime damage.

right-wing A right wing person or group supports the ideas and beliefs of capitalism.

satellite states Countries that are under the control of another country.

SLBM Submarine launched ballistic missile.

the Stasi The East German secret police.

trade embargo A punishment that prevents a country trading with other countries.

trade union Organised body of workers.

ultimatum A forceful demand, which leads to some form of retaliation if rejected.

US Secretary of State A senior government official mostly concerned with foreign policy.

SCHOLASTIC

Achieve the highest grades in **GCSE 9–1**

NEED MORE PRACTICE?

Don't worry, we've got plenty more GCSE revision and practice guides to help! In fact, we provide a range of essential GCSE 9–1 support for most popular subjects

Revision Guides

Broken down by topic, clearly laid out and packed with tools to study on the go – these are revision books that you can trust!

Study Guides

These detailed guides will help you get to know your English Literature set texts and History studies inside out!

Exam Practice Books

Packed full of questions to test your knowledge and at least one complete practice paper written by an exam expert.

Combined practice and revision books are also available from www.scholastic.co.uk/gcse

Plus... the free revision app

Download now from the App Store or Google Play so that you can revise wherever you want, whenever you want!

AVAILABLE FOR:

English Language | English Literature | Spelling, Punctuation & Grammar
Geography | Maths | Biology | Chemistry | Physics | Combined Science

Edexcel | AQA | All Boards